Cambridge IELTS 6

*Examination papers from
University of Cambridge
ESOL Examinations:
English for Speakers
of Other Languages*

CAMBRIDGE
UNIVERSITY PRESS

CAMBRIDGE UNIVERSITY PRESS
Cambridge, New York, Melbourne, Madrid, Cape Town,
Singapore, São Paulo, Delhi, Mexico City

Cambridge University Press
The Edinburgh Building, Cambridge CB2 8RU, UK

www.cambridge.org
Information on this title: www.cambridge.org/9780521693073

First published 2007
8th printing 2012

Printed and bound in the United Kingdom by the MPG Books Group

A catalogue record for this publication is available from the British Library

ISBN 978-0-521-69307-3 Student's Book with answers
ISBN 978-0-521-69310-3 Audio CDs (2)
ISBN 978-0-521-69309-7 Audio Cassettes (2)
ISBN 978-0-521-69308-0 Self-study Pack (Student's Book with answers and Audio CDs (2))

Cambridge University Press has no responsibility for the persistence or
accuracy of URLs for external or third-party internet websites referred to in
this publication, and does not guarantee that any content on such websites is,
or will remain, accurate or appropriate. Information regarding prices, travel
timetables and other factual information given in this work is correct at
the time of first printing but Cambridge University Press does not guarantee
the accuracy of such information thereafter.

Contents

Introduction

The International English Language Testing System (IELTS) is widely recognised as a reliable means of assessing the language ability of candidates who need to study or work where English is the language of communication. These Practice Tests are designed to give future IELTS candidates an idea of whether their English is at the required level.

IELTS is owned by three partners: the University of Cambridge ESOL Examinations, the British Council and IDP: Education Australia (through its subsidiary company, IELTS Australia Pty Limited). Further information on IELTS can be found on the IELTS website (www.ielts.org).

WHAT IS THE TEST FORMAT?

IELTS consists of six modules. All candidates take the same Listening and Speaking modules. There is a choice of Reading and Writing modules according to whether a candidate is taking the Academic or General Training version of the test.

Academic	General Training
For candidates taking the test for entry to undergraduate or postgraduate studies or for professional reasons.	For candidates taking the test for entry to vocational or training programmes not at degree level, for admission to secondary schools and for immigration purposes.

The test modules are taken in the following order:

Listening 4 sections, 40 items approximately 30 minutes		
Academic Reading 3 sections, 40 items 60 minutes	OR	**General Training Reading** 3 sections, 40 items 60 minutes
Academic Writing 2 tasks 60 minutes	OR	**General Training Writing** 2 tasks 60 minutes
Speaking 11 to 14 minutes		
Total Test Time 2 hours 44 minutes		

Listening

This module consists of four sections, each with ten questions. The first two sections are concerned with social needs. The first section is a conversation between two speakers and the second section is a monologue. The final two sections are concerned with situations related to educational or training contexts. The third section is a conversation between up to four people and the fourth section a monologue.

A variety of question types is used, including: multiple choice, short-answer questions, sentence completion, notes/form/table/summary/flow-chart completion, labelling a diagram/plan/map, classification, matching.

Candidates hear the recording once only and answer the questions as they listen. Ten minutes are allowed at the end for candidates to transfer their answers to the answer sheet.

Academic Reading

This module consists of three sections with 40 questions. There are three reading passages, which are taken from magazines, journals, books and newspapers. The passages are on topics of general interest. At least one passage contains detailed logical argument.

A variety of question types is used, including: multiple choice, short-answer questions, sentence completion, notes/summary/flow-chart/table completion, labelling a diagram, classification, matching, choosing suitable paragraph headings from a list, identification of writer's views/claims – *yes, no, not given* – or identification of information in the passage – *true, false, not given.*

General Training Reading

This module consists of three sections with 40 questions. The texts are taken from notices, advertisements, leaflets, newspapers, instruction manuals, books and magazines. The first section contains texts relevant to basic linguistic survival in English, with tasks mainly concerned with providing factual information. The second section focuses on the training context and involves texts of more complex language. The third section involves reading more extended texts, with a more complex structure, but with the emphasis on descriptive and instructive rather than argumentative texts.

A variety of question types is used, including: multiple choice, short-answer questions, sentence completion, notes/summary/flow-chart/table completion, labelling a diagram, classification, matching, choosing suitable paragraph headings from a list, identification of writer's views/claims – *yes, no, not given* – identification of information in the text – *true, false, not given.*

Academic Writing

This module consists of two tasks. It is suggested that candidates spend about 20 minutes on Task 1, which requires them to write at least 150 words, and 40 minutes on Task 2, which requires them to write at least 250 words. The assessment of Task 2 carries more weight in marking than Task 1.

Task 1 requires candidates to look at a diagram or some data (graph, table or chart) and to present the information in their own words. They are assessed on their ability to organise, present and possibly compare data, describe the stages of a process, describe an object or event, or explain how something works.

In Task 2 candidates are presented with a point of view, argument or problem. They are assessed on their ability to present a solution to the problem, present and justify an opinion, compare and contrast evidence and opinions, and evaluate and challenge ideas, evidence or arguments.

Candidates are also assessed on their ability to write in an appropriate style.

General Training Writing

This module consists of two tasks. It is suggested that candidates spend about 20 minutes on Task 1, which requires them to write at least 150 words, and 40 minutes on Task 2, which requires them to write at least 250 words. The assessment of Task 2 carries more weight in marking than Task 1.

In Task 1 candidates are asked to respond to a given problem with a letter requesting information or explaining a situation. They are assessed on their ability to engage in personal correspondence, elicit and provide general factual information, express needs, wants, likes and dislikes, express opinions, complaints, etc.

In Task 2 candidates are presented with a point of view, argument or problem. They are assessed on their ability to provide general factual information, outline a problem and present a solution, present and justify an opinion, and evaluate and challenge ideas, evidence or arguments.

Candidates are also judged on their ability to write in an appropriate style. More information on assessing both the Academic and General Training Writing modules, including Writing Band Descriptors (public version), is available on the IELTS website.

Speaking

This module takes between 11 and 14 minutes and is conducted by a trained examiner.

There are three parts:

Part 1
The candidate and the examiner introduce themselves. Candidates then answer general questions about themselves, their home/family, their job/studies, their interests and a wide range of similar familiar topic areas. This part lasts between four and five minutes.

Part 2
The candidate is given a task card with prompts and is asked to talk on a particular topic. The candidate has one minute to prepare and they can make some notes if they wish, before speaking for between one and two minutes. The examiner then asks one or two rounding-off questions.

Part 3
The examiner and the candidate engage in a discussion of more abstract issues which are thematically linked to the topic prompt in Part 2. The discussion lasts between four and five minutes.

The Speaking module assesses whether candidates can communicate effectively in English. The assessment takes into account Fluency and Coherence, Lexical Resource, Grammatical

Range and Accuracy, and Pronunciation. More information on assessing the Speaking module, including Speaking Band Descriptors (public version), is available on the IELTS website.

HOW IS IELTS SCORED?

IELTS results are reported on a nine-band scale. In addition to the score for overall language ability, IELTS provides a score in the form of a profile for each of the four skills (Listening, Reading, Writing and Speaking). These scores are also reported on a nine-band scale. All scores are recorded on the Test Report Form along with details of the candidate's nationality, first language and date of birth. Each Overall Band Score corresponds to a descriptive statement which gives a summary of the English language ability of a candidate classified at that level. The nine bands and their descriptive statements are as follows:

9 **Expert User** – *Has fully operational command of the language: appropriate, accurate and fluent with complete understanding.*

8 **Very Good User** – *Has fully operational command of the language with only occasional unsystematic inaccuracies and inappropriacies. Misunderstandings may occur in unfamiliar situations. Handles complex detailed argumentation well.*

7 **Good User** – *Has operational command of the language, though with occasional inaccuracies, inappropriacies and misunderstandings in some situations. Generally handles complex language well and understands detailed reasoning.*

6 **Competent User** – *Has generally effective command of the language despite some inaccuracies, inappropriacies and misunderstandings. Can use and understand fairly complex language, particularly in familiar situations.*

5 **Modest User** – *Has partial command of the language, coping with overall meaning in most situations, though is likely to make many mistakes. Should be able to handle basic communication in own field.*

4 **Limited User** – *Basic competence is limited to familiar situations. Has frequent problems in understanding and expression. Is not able to use complex language.*

3 **Extremely Limited User** – *Conveys and understands only general meaning in very familiar situations. Frequent breakdowns in communication occur.*

2 **Intermittent User** – *No real communication is possible except for the most basic information using isolated words or short formulae in familiar situations and to meet immediate needs. Has great difficulty understanding spoken and written English.*

1 **Non User** – *Essentially has no ability to use the language beyond possibly a few isolated words.*

0 **Did not attempt the test**. – *No assessable information provided.*

Most universities and colleges in the United Kingdom, Australia, New Zealand, Canada and the USA accept an IELTS Overall Band Score of 6.0–7.0 for entry to academic programmes.

MARKING THE PRACTICE TESTS

Listening and Reading

The Answer key is on pages 151–160.
Each question in the Listening and Reading modules is worth one mark.

Questions which require letter/Roman numeral answers
- For questions where the answers are letters or numbers, you should write *only* the number of answers required. For example, if the answer is a single letter or number you should write only one answer. If you have written more letters or numerals than are required, the answer must be marked wrong.

Questions which require answers in the form of words or numbers
- Answers may be written in upper or lower case.
- Words in brackets are *optional* – they are correct, but not necessary.
- Alternative answers are separated by a slash (/).
- If you are asked to write an answer using a certain number of words and/or (a) number(s), you will be penalised if you exceed this. For example, if a question specifies an answer using NO MORE THAN THREE WORDS and the correct answer is 'black leather coat', the answer of 'coat of black leather' is *incorrect*.
- In questions where you are expected to complete a gap, you should transfer only the necessary missing word(s) onto the answer sheet. For example, to complete 'in the . . .', and the correct answer is 'morning', the answer 'in the morning' would be *incorrect*.
- All answers require correct spelling (including words in brackets).
- Both US and UK spelling are acceptable and are included in the Answer key.
- All standard alternatives for numbers, dates and currencies are acceptable.
- All standard abbreviations are acceptable.
- You will find additional notes about individual questions in the Answer key.

Writing

It is not possible for you to give yourself a mark for the Writing tasks. For *Task 1* in *Tests 1* and *3*, and *Task 2* in *Tests 2* and *4*, and for *Task 1* in *General Training Test A* and *Task 2* in *General Training Test B*, we have provided *model answers* (written by an examiner) at the back of the book. It is important to note that these show just one way of completing the task, out of many possible approaches. For *Task 2* in *Tests 1* and *3*, *Task 1* in *Tests 2* and *4* and for *Task 2* in *General Training Test A* and *Task 1* in *General Training Test B*, we have provided *sample answers* (written by candidates), showing their score and the examiner's comments. These model answers and sample answers will give you an insight into what is required for the Writing module.

HOW SHOULD YOU INTERPRET YOUR SCORES?

In the Answer key at the end of each set of Listening and Reading answers you will find a chart which will help you assess whether, on the basis of your Practice Test results, you are ready to take the IELTS test.

In interpreting your score, there are a number of points you should bear in mind. Your performance in the real IELTS test will be reported in two ways: there will be a Band Score from 1 to 9 for each of the modules and an Overall Band Score from 1 to 9, which is the average of your scores in the four modules. However, institutions considering your application are advised to look at both the Overall Band and the Bands for each module in order to determine whether you have the language skills needed for a particular course of study. For example, if your course has a lot of reading and writing, but no lectures, listening skills might be less important and a score of 5 in Listening might be acceptable if the Overall Band Score was 7. However, for a course which has lots of lectures and spoken instructions, a score of 5 in Listening might be unacceptable even though the Overall Band Score was 7.

Once you have marked your tests you should have some idea of whether your listening and reading skills are good enough for you to try the IELTS test. If you did well enough in one module but not in others, you will have to decide for yourself whether you are ready to take the test.

The Practice Tests have been checked to ensure that they are of approximately the same level of difficulty as the real IELTS test. However, we cannot guarantee that your score in the Practice Tests will be reflected in the real IELTS test. The Practice Tests can only give you an idea of your possible future performance and it is ultimately up to you to make decisions based on your score.

Different institutions accept different IELTS scores for different types of courses. We have based our recommendations on the average scores which the majority of institutions accept. The institution to which you are applying may, of course, require a higher or lower score than most other institutions.

Sample answers and model answers are provided for the Writing tasks. The sample answers were written by IELTS candidates; each answer has been given a band score and the candidate's performance is described. Please note that there are many different ways by which a candidate may achieve a particular band score. The model answers were written by an examiner as examples of very good answers, but it is important to understand that they are just one example out of many possible approaches.

Further information

For more information about IELTS or any other University of Cambridge ESOL examination write to:

University of Cambridge ESOL Examinations
1 Hills Road
Cambridge
CB1 2EU
United Kingdom

Telephone: +44 1223 553355
Fax: +44 1223 460278
e-mail: Esolhelpdesk@CambridgeEsol.org
http://www.cambridgeesol.org
http://www.ielts.org

Test 1

SECTION 1   *Questions 1–10*

Questions 1–4

Complete the notes below.

*Write **NO MORE THAN THREE WORDS** for each answer.*

Notes on sports club

Example	*Answer*
Name of club:	***Kingswell***

Facilities available:	Golf
	1 ....
	2 ....
Classes available:	• Kick-boxing
	• **3** ....
Additional facility:	**4** .... (restaurant opening soon)

Questions 5–8

Complete the table below.

*Write **NO MORE THAN TWO NUMBERS** for each answer.*

MEMBERSHIP SCHEMES					
Type	**Use of facilities**	**Cost of classes**	**Times**	**Joining fee**	**Annual subscription fee**
GOLD	All	Free	Any time	£250	**5** £ ....
SILVER	All	**6** £	from **7** .... to	£225	£300
BRONZE	Restricted	£3	from 10.30 to 3.30 weekdays only	£50	**8** £ ....

Questions 9 and 10

Complete the sentences below.

*Write **ONE WORD ONLY** for each answer.*

9   To join the centre, you need to book an instructor's ....

10   To book a trial session, speak to David .... (0458 95311).

SECTION 2   *Questions 11–20*

Questions 11–16

What change has been made to each part of the theatre?

*Choose **SIX** answers from the box and write the correct letter, **A–G**, next to questions 11–16.*

RIVENDEN CITY THEATRE

A doubled in number
B given separate entrance
C reduced in number
D increased in size
E replaced
F strengthened
G temporarily closed

Part of the theatre

11	box office	....
12	shop	....
13	ordinary seats	....
14	seats for wheelchair users	....
15	lifts	....
16	dressing rooms	....

Questions 17–20

Complete the table below.

Write **NO MORE THAN TWO WORDS AND/OR A NUMBER** *for each answer.*

Play	Dates	Starting time	Tickets available	Price
Royal Hunt of the Sun	October 13th to **17**	**18** .... pm	for **19** .... and	**20** £ ....

SECTION 3   *Questions 21–30*

Question 21

*Choose the correct letter, **A**, **B** or **C**.*

21   What is Brian going to do before the course starts?

    A   attend a class

    B   write a report

    C   read a book

Questions 22–25

Complete the table below.

*Write **NO MORE THAN TWO WORDS** for each answer.*

College Facility	Information
Refectory	inform them **22** .... about special dietary requirements
23	long waiting list, apply now
Careers advice	drop-in centre for information
Fitness centre	reduced **24** .... for students
Library	includes books, journals, equipment room containing audio-visual materials
Computers	ask your **25** .... to arrange a password with the technical support team

Questions 26–30

Complete the summary below.

*Write **NO MORE THAN TWO WORDS** for each answer.*

Business Centre

The Business Resource Centre contains materials such as books and manuals to be used for training. It is possible to hire 26 .... and 27 .... There are materials for working on study skills (e.g. 28 ....) and other subjects include finance and 29 ....

30 .... membership costs £50 per year.

SECTION 4   *Questions 31–40*

Questions 31–37

Complete the table below.

*Write **NO MORE THAN TWO WORDS** for each answer.*

Social history of the East End of London

Period	Situation
1st–4th centuries	Produce from the area was used to **31**......................... the people of London.
5th–10th centuries	New technology allowed the production of goods made of **32** .... and ....
11th century	Lack of **33** .... in the East End encouraged the growth of businesses.
16th century	Construction of facilities for the building of **34** .... stimulated international trade. Agricultural workers came from other parts of **35** .... to look for work.
17th century	Marshes were drained to provide land that could be **36** .... on.
19th century	Inhabitants lived in conditions of great **37** .... with very poor sanitation.

Questions 38–40

Choose **THREE** *letters, A–G.*

Which **THREE** of the following problems are mentioned in connection with 20th century housing in the East End?

    A   unsympathetic landlords

    B   unclean water

    C   heating problems

    D   high rents

    E   overcrowding

    F   poor standards of building

    G   houses catching fire

READING

READING PASSAGE 1

You should spend about 20 minutes on **Questions 1–13**, *which are based on Reading Passage 1 below.*

AUSTRALIA'S SPORTING SUCCESS

A   They play hard, they play often, and they play to win. Australian sports teams win more than their fair share of titles, demolishing rivals with seeming ease. How do they do it? A big part of the secret is an extensive and expensive network of sporting academies underpinned by science and medicine. At the Australian Institute of Sport (AIS), hundreds of youngsters and pros live and train under the eyes of coaches. Another body, the Australian Sports Commission (ASC), finances programmes of excellence in a total of 96 sports for thousands of sportsmen and women. Both provide intensive coaching, training facilities and nutritional advice.

B   Inside the academies, science takes centre stage. The AIS employs more than 100 sports scientists and doctors, and collaborates with scores of others in universities and research centres. AIS scientists work across a number of sports, applying skills learned in one – such as building muscle strength in golfers – to others, such as swimming and squash. They are backed up by technicians who design instruments to collect data from athletes. They all focus on one aim: winning. 'We can't waste our time looking at ethereal scientific questions that don't help the coach work with an athlete and improve performance,' says Peter Fricker, chief of science at AIS.

C   A lot of their work comes down to measurement – everything from the exact angle of a swimmer's dive to the second-by-second power output of a cyclist. This data is used to wring improvements out of athletes. The focus is on individuals, tweaking performances to squeeze an extra hundredth of a second here, an extra millimetre there. No gain is too slight to bother with. It's the tiny, gradual improvements that add up to world-beating results. To demonstrate how the system works, Bruce Mason at AIS shows off the prototype of a 3D analysis tool for studying swimmers. A wire-frame model of a champion swimmer slices through the water, her arms moving in slow motion. Looking side-on, Mason measures the distance between strokes. From above, he analyses how her spine swivels. When fully developed, this system will enable him to build a biomechanical profile for coaches to use to help budding swimmers. Mason's contribution to sport also includes the development of the SWAN (SWimming ANalysis) system now used in Australian national competitions. It collects images from digital cameras running at 50 frames a second and breaks down each part of a swimmer's performance into factors that can be analysed individually – stroke length, stroke frequency, average duration of each stroke, velocity, start, lap and finish times, and so on. At the end of each race, SWAN spits out data on each swimmer.

D 'Take a look,' says Mason, pulling out a sheet of data. He points out the data on the swimmers in second and third place, which shows that the one who finished third actually swam faster. So why did he finish 35 hundredths of a second down? 'His turn times were 44 hundredths of a second behind the other guy,' says Mason. 'If he can improve on his turns, he can do much better.' This is the kind of accuracy that AIS scientists' research is bringing to a range of sports. With the Cooperative Research Centre for Micro Technology in Melbourne, they are developing unobtrusive sensors that will be embedded in an athlete's clothes or running shoes to monitor heart rate, sweating, heat production or any other factor that might have an impact on an athlete's ability to run. There's more to it than simply measuring performance. Fricker gives the example of athletes who may be down with coughs and colds 11 or 12 times a year. After years of experimentation, AIS and the University of Newcastle in New South Wales developed a test that measures how much of the immune-system protein immunoglobulin A is present in athletes' saliva. If IgA levels suddenly fall below a certain level, training is eased or dropped altogether. Soon, IgA levels start rising again, and the danger passes. Since the tests were introduced, AIS athletes in all sports have been remarkably successful at staying healthy.

E Using data is a complex business. Well before a championship, sports scientists and coaches start to prepare the athlete by developing a 'competition model', based on what they expect will be the winning times. 'You design the model to make *that* time,' says Mason. 'A start of *this* much, each free-swimming period has to be *this* fast, with a certain stroke frequency and stroke length, with turns done in *these* times.' All the training is then geared towards making the athlete hit those targets, both overall and for each segment of the race. Techniques like these have transformed Australia into arguably the world's most successful sporting nation.

F Of course, there's nothing to stop other countries copying – and many have tried. Some years ago, the AIS unveiled coolant-lined jackets for endurance athletes. At the Atlanta Olympic Games in 1996, these sliced as much as two per cent off cyclists' and rowers' times. Now everyone uses them. The same has happened to the 'altitude tent', developed by AIS to replicate the effect of altitude training at sea level. But Australia's success story is about more than easily copied technological fixes, and up to now no nation has replicated its all-encompassing system.

Questions 1–7

Reading Passage 1 has six paragraphs, **A–F**.

Which paragraph contains the following information?

*Write the correct letter, **A–F**, in boxes 1–7 on your answer sheet.*

NB   You may use any letter more than once.

1   a reference to the exchange of expertise between different sports

2   an explanation of how visual imaging is employed in investigations

3   a reason for narrowing the scope of research activity

4   how some AIS ideas have been reproduced

5   how obstacles to optimum achievement can be investigated

6   an overview of the funded support of athletes

7   how performance requirements are calculated before an event

Questions 8–11

Classify the following techniques according to whether the writer states they

>   **A**   *are currently exclusively used by Australians*
>   **B**   *will be used in the future by Australians*
>   **C**   *are currently used by both Australians and their rivals*

*Write the correct letter, **A, B** or **C**, in boxes 8–11 on your answer sheet.*

8   cameras

9   sensors

10   protein tests

11   altitude tents

Questions 12 and 13

Answer the questions below.

Choose **NO MORE THAN THREE WORDS AND/OR A NUMBER** *from the passage for each answer.*

Write your answers in boxes 12 and 13 on your answer sheet.

12   What is produced to help an athlete plan their performance in an event?

13   By how much did some cyclists' performance improve at the 1996 Olympic Games?

READING PASSAGE 2

*You should spend about 20 minutes on **Questions 14–26**, which are based on Reading Passage 2 below.*

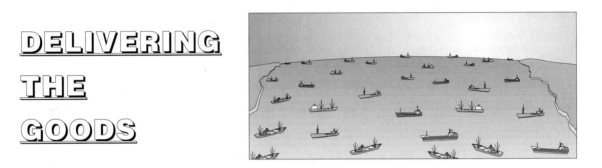

DELIVERING THE GOODS

The vast expansion in international trade owes much to a revolution in the business of moving freight

A International trade is growing at a startling pace. While the global economy has been expanding at a bit over 3% a year, the volume of trade has been rising at a compound annual rate of about twice that. Foreign products, from meat to machinery, play a more important role in almost every economy in the world, and foreign markets now tempt businesses that never much worried about sales beyond their nation's borders.

B What lies behind this explosion in international commerce? The general worldwide decline in trade barriers, such as customs duties and import quotas, is surely one explanation. The economic opening of countries that have traditionally been minor players is another. But one force behind the import–export boom has passed all but unnoticed: the rapidly falling cost of getting goods to market. Theoretically, in the world of trade, shipping costs do not matter. Goods, once they have been made, are assumed to move instantly and at no cost from place to place. The real world, however, is full of frictions. Cheap labour may make Chinese clothing competitive in America, but if delays in shipment tie up working capital and cause winter coats to arrive in spring, trade may lose its advantages.

C At the turn of the 20th century, agriculture and manufacturing were the two most important sectors almost everywhere, accounting for about 70% of total output in Germany, Italy and France, and 40–50% in America, Britain and Japan. International commerce was therefore dominated by raw materials, such as wheat, wood and iron ore, or processed commodities, such as meat and steel. But these sorts of products are heavy and bulky and the cost of transporting them relatively high.

D Countries still trade disproportionately with their geographic neighbours. Over time, however, world output has shifted into goods whose worth is unrelated to their size and weight. Today, it is finished manufactured products that dominate the flow of trade, and, thanks to technological advances such as lightweight components, manufactured goods themselves have tended to become lighter and less bulky. As a result, less transportation is required for every dollar's worth of imports or exports.

E   To see how this influences trade, consider the business of making disk drives for computers. Most of the world's disk-drive manufacturing is concentrated in South-east Asia. This is possible only because disk drives, while valuable, are small and light and so cost little to ship. Computer manufacturers in Japan or Texas will not face hugely bigger freight bills if they import drives from Singapore rather than purchasing them on the domestic market. Distance therefore poses no obstacle to the globalisation of the disk-drive industry.

F   This is even more true of the fast-growing information industries. Films and compact discs cost little to transport, even by aeroplane. Computer software can be 'exported' without ever loading it onto a ship, simply by transmitting it over telephone lines from one country to another, so freight rates and cargo-handling schedules become insignificant factors in deciding where to make the product. Businesses can locate based on other considerations, such as the availability of labour, while worrying less about the cost of delivering their output.

G   In many countries deregulation has helped to drive the process along. But, behind the scenes, a series of technological innovations known broadly as *containerisation* and *inter-modal transportation* has led to swift productivity improvements in cargo-handling. Forty years ago, the process of exporting or importing involved a great many stages of handling, which risked portions of the shipment being damaged or stolen along the way. The invention of the container crane made it possible to load and unload containers without capsizing the ship and the adoption of standard container sizes allowed almost any box to be transported on any ship. By 1967, dual-purpose ships, carrying loose cargo in the hold* and containers on the deck, were giving way to all-container vessels that moved thousands of boxes at a time.

H   The shipping container transformed ocean shipping into a highly efficient, intensely competitive business. But getting the cargo to and from the dock was a different story. National governments, by and large, kept a much firmer hand on truck and railroad tariffs than on charges for ocean freight. This started changing, however, in the mid-1970s, when America began to deregulate its transportation industry. First airlines, then road hauliers and railways, were freed from restrictions on what they could carry, where they could haul it and what price they could charge. Big productivity gains resulted. Between 1985 and 1996, for example, America's freight railways dramatically reduced their employment, trackage, and their fleets of locomotives – while increasing the amount of cargo they hauled. Europe's railways have also shown marked, albeit smaller, productivity improvements.

I   In America the period of huge productivity gains in transportation may be almost over, but in most countries the process still has far to go. State ownership of railways and airlines, regulation of freight rates and toleration of anti-competitive practices, such as cargo-handling monopolies, all keep the cost of shipping unnecessarily high and deter international trade. Bringing these barriers down would help the world's economies grow even closer.

----

* *hold:* ship's storage area below deck

Questions 14–17

Reading Passage 2 has nine paragraphs, **A–I**.

Which paragraph contains the following information?

*Write the correct letter, **A–I**, in boxes 14–17 on your answer sheet.*

14   a suggestion for improving trade in the future

15   the effects of the introduction of electronic delivery

16   the similar cost involved in transporting a product from abroad or from a local supplier

17   the weakening relationship between the value of goods and the cost of their delivery

Questions 18–22

Do the following statements agree with the information given in Reading Passage 2?

In boxes 18–22 on your answer sheet, write

> **TRUE**   *if the statement agrees with the information*
> **FALSE**   *if the statement contradicts the information*
> **NOT GIVEN**   *if there is no information on this*

18   International trade is increasing at a greater rate than the world economy.

19   Cheap labour guarantees effective trade conditions.

20   Japan imports more meat and steel than France.

21   Most countries continue to prefer to trade with nearby nations.

22   Small computer components are manufactured in Germany.

Questions 23–26

*Complete the summary using the list of words, **A–K**, below.*

*Write the correct letter, **A–K**, in boxes 23–26 on your answer sheet.*

THE TRANSPORT REVOLUTION

Modern cargo-handling methods have had a significant effect on **23** .... as the business of moving freight around the world becomes increasingly streamlined. Manufacturers of computers, for instance, are able to import **24** ....

from overseas, rather than having to rely on a local supplier. The introduction of

25 .... has meant that bulk cargo can be safely and efficiently moved over long distances. While international shipping is now efficient, there is still a need for governments to reduce **26** .... in order to free up the domestic cargo sector.

A	tariffs	**B**	components	**C**	container ships
D	output	**E**	employees	**F**	insurance costs
G	trade	**H**	freight	**I**	fares
J	software	**K**	international standards		

READING PASSAGE 3

*You should spend about 20 minutes on **Questions 27–40**, which are based on Reading Passage 3 on the following pages.*

Questions 27–32

Reading Passage 3 has seven paragraphs, **A–G**.

*Choose the correct heading for paragraphs **B–G** from the list of headings below.*

*Write the correct number, **i–ix**, in boxes 27–32 on your answer sheet.*

List of Headings

i	The reaction of the Inuit community to climate change
ii	Understanding of climate change remains limited
iii	Alternative sources of essential supplies
iv	Respect for Inuit opinion grows
v	A healthier choice of food
vi	A difficult landscape
vii	Negative effects on well-being
viii	Alarm caused by unprecedented events in the Arctic
ix	The benefits of an easier existence

Example	*Answer*
Paragraph **A**	**viii**

---

27 Paragraph **B**

28 Paragraph **C**

29 Paragraph **D**

30 Paragraph **E**

31 Paragraph **F**

32 Paragraph **G**

Climate Change and the Inuit

The threat posed by climate change in the Arctic and the problems faced by Canada's Inuit people

A Unusual incidents are being reported across the Arctic. Inuit families going off on snowmobiles to prepare their summer hunting camps have found themselves cut off from home by a sea of mud, following early thaws. There are reports of igloos losing their insulating properties as the snow drips and refreezes, of lakes draining into the sea as permafrost melts, and sea ice breaking up earlier than usual, carrying seals beyond the reach of hunters. Climate change may still be a rather abstract idea to most of us, but in the Arctic it is already having dramatic effects – if summertime ice continues to shrink at its present rate, the Arctic Ocean could soon become virtually ice-free in summer. The knock-on effects are likely to include more warming, cloudier skies, increased precipitation and higher sea levels. Scientists are increasingly keen to find out what's going on because they consider the Arctic the 'canary in the mine' for global warming – a warning of what's in store for the rest of the world.

B For the Inuit the problem is urgent. They live in precarious balance with one of the toughest environments on earth. Climate change, whatever its causes, is a direct threat to their way of life. Nobody knows the Arctic as well as the locals, which is why they are not content simply to stand back and let outside experts tell them what's happening. In Canada, where the Inuit people are jealously guarding their hard-won autonomy in the country's newest territory, Nunavut, they believe their best hope of survival in this changing environment lies in combining their ancestral knowledge with the best of modern science. This is a challenge in itself.

C The Canadian Arctic is a vast, treeless polar desert that's covered with snow for most of the year. Venture into this terrain and you get some idea of the hardships facing anyone who calls this home. Farming is out of the question and nature offers meagre pickings. Humans first settled in the Arctic a mere 4,500 years ago, surviving by exploiting sea mammals and fish. The environment tested them to the limits: sometimes the colonists were successful, sometimes they failed and vanished. But around a thousand years ago, one group emerged that was uniquely well adapted to cope with the Arctic environment. These Thule people moved in from Alaska, bringing kayaks, sleds, dogs, pottery and iron tools. They are the ancestors of today's Inuit people.

D Life for the descendants of the Thule people is still harsh. Nunavut is 1.9 million square kilometres of rock and ice, and a handful of islands around the North Pole. It's currently home to 2,500 people, all but a handful of them indigenous Inuit. Over the past 40 years, most have abandoned their nomadic ways and settled in the territory's 28 isolated communities, but they still rely heavily on nature to provide food and clothing.

Provisions available in local shops have to be flown into Nunavut on one of the most costly air networks in the world, or brought by supply ship during the few ice-free weeks of summer. It would cost a family around £7,000 a year to replace meat they obtained themselves through hunting with imported meat. Economic opportunities are scarce, and for many people state benefits are their only income.

E While the Inuit may not actually starve if hunting and trapping are curtailed by climate change, there has certainly been an impact on people's health. Obesity, heart disease and diabetes are beginning to appear in a people for whom these have never before been problems. There has been a crisis of identity as the traditional skills of hunting, trapping and preparing skins have begun to disappear. In Nunavut's 'igloo and email' society, where adults who were born in igloos have children who may never have been out on the land, there's a high incidence of depression.

F With so much at stake, the Inuit are determined to play a key role in teasing out the mysteries of climate change in the Arctic. Having survived there for centuries, they believe their wealth of traditional knowledge is vital to the task. And Western scientists are starting to draw on this wisdom, increasingly referred to as 'Inuit Qaujimajatuqangit', or IQ. 'In the early days scientists ignored us when they came up here to study anything. They just figured these people don't know very much so we won't ask them,' says John Amagoalik, an Inuit leader and politician. 'But in recent years IQ has had much more credibility and weight.' In fact it is now a requirement for anyone hoping to get permission to do research that they consult the communities, who are helping to set the research agenda to reflect their most important concerns. They can turn down applications from scientists they believe will work against their interests, or research projects that will impinge too much on their daily lives and traditional activities.

G Some scientists doubt the value of traditional knowledge because the occupation of the Arctic doesn't go back far enough. Others, however, point out that the first weather stations in the far north date back just 50 years. There are still huge gaps in our environmental knowledge, and despite the scientific onslaught, many predictions are no more than best guesses. IQ could help to bridge the gap and resolve the tremendous uncertainty about how much of what we're seeing is natural capriciousness and how much is the consequence of human activity.

Questions 33–40

Complete the summary of paragraphs C and D below.

*Choose **NO MORE THAN TWO WORDS** from paragraphs C and D for each answer.*

Write your answers in boxes 33–40 on your answer sheet.

If you visit the Canadian Arctic, you immediately appreciate the problems faced by people for whom this is home. It would clearly be impossible for the people to engage in 33 .... as a means of supporting themselves. For thousands of years they have had to rely on catching 34 .... and 35 .... as a means of sustenance. The harsh surroundings saw many who tried to settle there pushed to their limits, although some were successful. The 36 .... people were an example of the latter and for them the environment did not prove unmanageable. For the present inhabitants, life continues to be a struggle. The territory of Nunavut consists of little more than ice, rock and a few 37 .... In recent years, many of them have been obliged to give up their 38 .... lifestyle, but they continue to depend mainly on 39 .... for their food and clothes. 40 .... produce is particularly expensive.

WRITING

WRITING TASK 1

You should spend about 20 minutes on this task.

> *The graph and table below give information about water use worldwide and water consumption in two different countries.*
>
> *Summarise the information by selecting and reporting the main features, and make comparisons where relevant.*

Write at least 150 words.

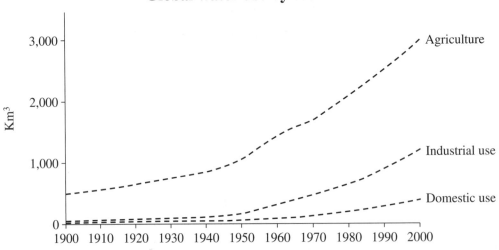

Global water use by sector

Water consumption in Brazil and Congo in 2000

Country	Population	Irrigated land	Water consumption per person
Brazil	176 million	26,500 km^2	359 m^3
Democractic Republic of Congo	5.2 million	100 km^2	8 m^3

WRITING TASK 2

You should spend about 40 minutes on this task.

Write about the following topic:

> *Today, the high sales of popular consumer goods reflect the power of advertising and not the real needs of the society in which they are sold.*
>
> *To what extent do you agree or disagree?*

Give reasons for your answer and include any relevant examples from your own knowledge or experience.

Write at least 250 words.

SPEAKING

PART 1

The examiner asks the candidate about him/herself, his/her home, work or studies and other familiar topics.

EXAMPLE

Dancing

- Do you enjoy dancing? [Why/Why not?]
- Has anyone ever taught you to dance? [Why/Why not?]
- Tell me about any traditional dancing in your country.
- Do you think that traditional dancing will be popular in the future? [Why/Why not?]

PART 2

Describe someone in your family who you like.

You should say:
  how this person is related to you
  what this person looks like
  what kind of person he/she is
and explain why you like this person.

You will have to talk about the topic for one to two minutes.
You have one minute to think about what you are going to say.
You can make some notes to help you if you wish.

PART 3

Discussion topics:

Family similarities

Example questions:
In what ways can people in a family be similar to each other?
Do you think that daughters are always more similar to mothers than to male relatives? What about sons and fathers?
In terms of personality, are people more influenced by their family or by their friends? In what ways?

Genetic research

Example questions:
Where can people in your country get information about genetic research?
How do people in your country feel about genetic research?
Should this research be funded by governments or private companies? Why?

Test 2

LISTENING

SECTION 1 *Questions 1–10*

Questions 1–5

Complete the notes below.

*Write **NO MORE THAN TWO WORDS AND/OR A NUMBER** for each answer.*

CHILDREN'S ART AND CRAFT WORKSHOPS

Example	*Answer*
Workshops organised every:	***Saturday***

- Adults must accompany children under **1** ....
- Cost: £2.50
- Workshops held in: Winter House, **2** .... Street
- Security device: must push the **3** .... to open door
- Should leave car behind the **4** ....
- Book workshops by phoning the **5** .... (on 200765)

Questions 6–10

Complete the table below.

*Write **NO MORE THAN TWO WORDS** for each answer.*

Next two workshops

Date	Workshop title	Children advised to wear:	Please bring (if possible):
16/11	'Building **6** ....'	**7**	**8** ....
23/11	**9** '........................'	(Nothing special)	**10** ....

SECTION 2   *Questions 11–20*

Questions 11–14

Complete the sentences below.

*Write **NO MORE THAN TWO WORDS AND/OR A NUMBER** for each answer.*

TRAIN INFORMATION

11   Local services depart from .... railway station.

12   National services depart from the .... railway station.

13   Trains for London depart every .... each day during the week.

14   The price of a first class ticket includes ....

Questions 15–17

Complete the table below.

*Write **NO MORE THAN TWO WORDS AND/OR A NUMBER** for each answer.*

Type of ticket	Details
Standard open	no restrictions
Supersave	travel after 8.45
Special	travel after **15** .... and at weekends
16	buy at least six days ahead limited numbers **17** .... essential

Questions 18–20

Choose **THREE** *letters, A–G.*

Which **THREE** attractions can you visit at present by train from Trebirch?

    A   a science museum

    B   a theme park

    C   a climbing wall

    D   a mining museum

    E   an aquarium

    F   a castle

    G   a zoo

SECTION 3   *Questions 21–30*

Complete the tables below.

*Write **NO MORE THAN THREE WORDS AND/OR A NUMBER** for each answer.*

Dissertation Tutorial Record (Education)

Name: Sandy Gibbons

Targets previously agreed	Work completed	Further action suggested
Investigate suitable data analysis software	– Read IT **21** .... – Spoken to Jane Prince, Head of the **22**	Sign up for some software practice sessions
Prepare a **23** .... for survey	– Completed and sent for review	Add questions in section three on **24** ....
Further reading about discipline	– Read Banerjee – N.B. Couldn't find Ericsson's essays on managing the **25**	Obtain from library through special loans service

New Targets	Specific suggestions	Timing
Do further work on Chapter 1 (Give the title: *Context* **26** ....)	– Add statistics on the **27** .... in various zones – Include more references to works dated after **28**	By the **29** ....
Prepare list of main sections for Chapter 2	– Use index cards to help in organisation	Before starting the **30** ....

SECTION 4   *Questions 31–40*

Questions 31–37

*Choose the correct letter, **A**, **B** or **C**.*

The history of moving pictures

31   Some photographs of a horse running showed

   A   all feet off the ground.
   B   at least one foot on the ground.
   C   two feet off the ground.

32   The Scotsman employed by Edison

   A   designed a system to use the technology Edison had invented.
   B   used available technology to make a new system.
   C   was already an expert in motion picture technology.

33   One major problem with the first system was that

   A   only one person could be filmed.
   B   people could only see very short films.
   C   the camera was very heavy.

34   Rival systems started to appear in Europe after people had

   A   been told about the American system.
   B   seen the American system.
   C   used the American system.

35   In 1895, a famous new system was developed by

   A   a French team working alone.
   B   a French and German team working together.
   C   a German team who invented the word 'cinema'.

36   Longer films were not made at the time because of problems involving

   A   the subject matter.
   B   the camera.
   C   the film projector.

37   The 'Lantham Loop' invention relied on

   A   removing tension between the film reels.
   B   adding three more film reels to the system.
   C   making one of the film reels more effective.

Questions 38–40

Complete the sentences below.

*Write **NO MORE THAN THREE WORDS** for each answer.*

38 The first motion picture was called *The* ....

39 .... were used for the first time on film in 1926.

40 Subtitles were added to *The Lights of New York* because of its ....

■ **READING** ■

READING PASSAGE 1

*You should spend about 20 minutes on **Questions 1–13**, which are based on Reading Passage 1 on the following pages.*

Questions 1–5

Reading Passage 1 has five marked paragraphs, **A–E**.

Choose the correct heading for each paragraph from the list of headings below.

*Write the correct number, **i–viii**, in boxes 1–5 on your answer sheet.*

List of Headings

i	Avoiding an overcrowded centre
ii	A successful exercise in people power
iii	The benefits of working together in cities
iv	Higher incomes need not mean more cars
v	Economic arguments fail to persuade
vi	The impact of telecommunications on population distribution
vii	Increases in travelling time
viii	Responding to arguments against public transport

---

1 Paragraph **A**

2 Paragraph **B**

3 Paragraph **C**

4 Paragraph **D**

5 Paragraph **E**

Advantages of public transport

A new study conducted for the World Bank by Murdoch University's Institute for Science and Technology Policy (ISTP) has demonstrated that public transport is more efficient than cars. The study compared the proportion of wealth poured into transport by thirty-seven cities around the world. This included both the public and private costs of building, maintaining and using a transport system.

The study found that the Western Australian city of Perth is a good example of a city with minimal public transport. As a result, 17% of its wealth went into transport costs. Some European and Asian cities, on the other hand, spent as little as 5%. Professor Peter Newman, ISTP Director, pointed out that these more efficient cities were able to put the difference into attracting industry and jobs or creating a better place to live.

According to Professor Newman, the larger Australian city of Melbourne is a rather unusual city in this sort of comparison. He describes it as two cities: 'A European city surrounded by a car-dependent one'. Melbourne's large tram network has made car use in the inner city much lower, but the outer suburbs have the same car-based structure as most other Australian cities. The explosion in demand for accommodation in the inner suburbs of Melbourne suggests a recent change in many people's preferences as to where they live.

Newman says this is a new, broader way of considering public transport issues. In the past, the case for public transport has been made on the basis of environmental and social justice considerations rather than economics. Newman, however, believes the study demonstrates that 'the auto-dependent city model is inefficient and grossly inadequate in economic as well as environmental terms'.

Bicycle use was not included in the study but Newman noted that the two most 'bicycle friendly' cities considered – Amsterdam and Copenhagen – were very efficient, even though their public transport systems were 'reasonable but not special'.

It is common for supporters of road networks to reject the models of cities with good public transport by arguing that such systems would not work in their particular city. One objection is climate. Some people say their city could not make more use of public transport because it is either too hot or too cold. Newman rejects this, pointing out that public transport has been successful in both Toronto and Singapore and, in fact, he has checked the use of cars against climate and found 'zero correlation'.

When it comes to other physical features, road lobbies are on stronger ground. For example, Newman accepts it would be hard for a city as hilly as Auckland to develop a really good rail network. However, he points out that both Hong Kong and Zürich have managed to make a success of their rail systems, heavy and light respectively, though there are few cities in the world as hilly.

A   In fact, Newman believes the main reason for adopting one sort of transport over another is politics: 'The more democratic the process, the more public transport is favored.' He considers Portland, Oregon, a perfect example of this. Some years ago, federal money was granted to build a new road. However, local pressure groups forced a referendum over whether to spend the money on light rail instead. The rail proposal won and the railway worked spectacularly well. In the years that have followed, more and more rail systems have been put in, dramatically changing the nature of the city. Newman notes that Portland has about the same population as Perth and had a similar population density at the time.

B   In the UK, travel times to work had been stable for at least six centuries, with people avoiding situations that required them to spend more than half an hour travelling to work. Trains and cars initially allowed people to live at greater distances without taking longer to reach their destination. However, public infrastructure did not keep pace with urban sprawl, causing massive congestion problems which now make commuting times far higher.

C   There is a widespread belief that increasing wealth encourages people to live farther out where cars are the only viable transport. The example of European cities refutes that. They are often wealthier than their American counterparts but have not generated the same level of car use. In Stockholm, car use has actually fallen in recent years as the city has become larger and wealthier. A new study makes this point even more starkly. Developing cities in Asia, such as Jakarta and Bangkok, make more use of the car than wealthy Asian cities such as Tokyo and Singapore. In cities that developed later, the World Bank and Asian Development Bank discouraged the building of public transport and people have been forced to rely on cars – creating the massive traffic jams that characterize those cities.

D   Newman believes one of the best studies on how cities built for cars might be converted to rail use is *The Urban Village* report, which used Melbourne as an example. It found that pushing everyone into the city centre was not the best approach. Instead, the proposal advocated the creation of urban villages at hundreds of sites, mostly around railway stations.

E   It was once assumed that improvements in telecommunications would lead to more dispersal in the population as people were no longer forced into cities. However, the ISTP team's research demonstrates that the population and job density of cities rose or remained constant in the 1980s after decades of decline. The explanation for this seems to be that it is valuable to place people working in related fields together. 'The new world will largely depend on human creativity, and creativity flourishes where people come together face-to-face.'

Questions 6–10

Do the following statements agree with the information given in Reading Passage 1?

In boxes 6–10 on your answer sheet, write

> **TRUE**   *if the statement agrees with the information*
> **FALSE**   *if the statement contradicts the information*
> **NOT GIVEN** *if there is no information on this*

6   The ISTP study examined public and private systems in every city of the world.

7   Efficient cities can improve the quality of life for their inhabitants.

8   An inner-city tram network is dangerous for car drivers.

9   In Melbourne, people prefer to live in the outer suburbs.

10   Cities with high levels of bicycle usage can be efficient even when public transport is only averagely good.

Questions 11–13

Look at the following cities (Questions 11–13) and the list of descriptions below.

*Match each city with the correct description, **A–F**.*

*Write the correct letter, **A–F**, in boxes 11–13 on your answer sheet.*

11   Perth

12   Auckland

13   Portland

List of Descriptions

A   successfully uses a light rail transport system in hilly environment
B   successful public transport system despite cold winters
C   profitably moved from road to light rail transport system
D   hilly and inappropriate for rail transport system
E   heavily dependent on cars despite widespread poverty
F   inefficient due to a limited public transport system

READING PASSAGE 2

*You should spend about 20 minutes on **Questions 14–26**, which are based on Reading Passage 2 below.*

GREYING POPULATION STAYS IN THE PINK

Elderly people are growing healthier, happier and more independent, say American scientists. The results of a 14-year study to be announced later this month reveal that the diseases associated with old age are afflicting fewer and fewer people and when they do strike, it is much later in life.

In the last 14 years, the National Long-term Health Care Survey has gathered data on the health and lifestyles of more than 20,000 men and women over 65. Researchers, now analysing the results of data gathered in 1994, say arthritis, high blood pressure and circulation problems – the major medical complaints in this age group – are troubling a smaller proportion every year. And the data confirms that the rate at which these diseases are declining continues to accelerate. Other diseases of old age – dementia, stroke, arteriosclerosis and emphysema – are also troubling fewer and fewer people.

'It really raises the question of what should be considered normal ageing,' says Kenneth Manton, a demographer from Duke University in North Carolina. He says the problems doctors accepted as normal in a 65-year-old in 1982 are often not appearing until people are 70 or 75.

Clearly, certain diseases are beating a retreat in the face of medical advances. But there may be other contributing factors. Improvements in childhood nutrition in the first quarter of the twentieth century, for example, gave today's elderly people a better start in life than their predecessors.

On the downside, the data also reveals failures in public health that have caused surges in some illnesses. An increase in some cancers and bronchitis may reflect changing smoking habits and poorer air quality, say the researchers. 'These may be subtle influences,' says Manton, 'but our subjects have been exposed to worse and worse pollution for over 60 years. It's not surprising we see some effect.'

One interesting correlation Manton uncovered is that better-educated people are likely to live longer. For example, 65-year-old women with fewer than eight years of schooling are expected, on average, to live to 82. Those who continued their education live an extra seven years. Although some of this can be attributed to a higher income, Manton believes it is mainly because educated people seek more medical attention.

The survey also assessed how independent people over 65 were, and again found a striking trend. Almost 80% of those in the 1994 survey could complete everyday activities ranging from eating and dressing unaided to complex tasks such as cooking and managing their finances. That represents a significant drop in the number of disabled old people in the population. If the trends apparent in the United States 14 years ago had continued, researchers calculate there would be an additional one million disabled elderly people in today's population. According to Manton, slowing the trend has saved the United States government's Medicare system more than $200 billion, suggesting that the greying of America's population may prove less of a financial burden than expected.

The increasing self-reliance of many elderly people is probably linked to a massive increase in the use of simple home medical aids. For instance, the use of raised toilet seats has more than doubled since the start of the study, and the use of bath seats has grown by more than 50%. These developments also bring some health benefits, according to a report from the MacArthur Foundation's research group on successful ageing. The group found that those elderly people who were able to retain a sense of independence were more likely to stay healthy in old age.

Maintaining a level of daily physical activity may help mental functioning, says Carl Cotman, a neuroscientist at the University of California at Irvine. He found that rats that exercise on a treadmill have raised levels of brain-derived neurotrophic factor coursing through their brains. Cotman believes this hormone, which keeps neurons functioning, may prevent the brains of active humans from deteriorating.

As part of the same study, Teresa Seeman, a social epidemiologist at the University of Southern California in Los Angeles, found a connection between self-esteem and stress in people over 70. In laboratory simulations of challenging activities such as driving, those who felt in control of their lives pumped out lower levels of stress hormones such as cortisol. Chronically high levels of these hormones have been linked to heart disease.

But independence can have drawbacks. Seeman found that elderly people who felt emotionally isolated maintained higher levels of stress hormones even when asleep. The research suggests that older people fare best when they feel independent but know they can get help when they need it.

'Like much research into ageing, these results support common sense,' says Seeman. They also show that we may be underestimating the impact of these simple factors. 'The sort of thing that your grandmother always told you turns out to be right on target,' she says.

Questions 14–22

*Complete the summary using the list of words, **A–Q**, below.*

*Write the correct letter, **A–Q**, in boxes 14–22 on your answer sheet.*

Research carried out by scientists in the United States has shown that the proportion of people over 65 suffering from the most common age-related medical problems is 14 .... and that the speed of this change is 15 .... It also seems that these diseases are affecting people 16 .... in life than they did in the past. This is largely due to developments in 17 .... , but other factors such as improved 18 .... may also be playing a part. Increases in some other illnesses may be due to changes in personal habits and to 19 .... The research establishes a link between levels of 20 .... and life expectancy. It also shows that there has been a considerable reduction in the number of elderly people who are 21 .... , which means that the 22 .... involved in supporting this section of the population may be less than previously predicted.

A cost	**B** falling	**C** technology
D undernourished	**E** earlier	**F** later
G disabled	**H** more	**I** increasing
J nutrition	**K** education	**L** constant
M medicine	**N** pollution	**O** environmental
P health	**Q** independent	

Questions 23–26

*Complete each sentence with the correct ending, **A–H**, below.*

*Write the correct letter, **A–H**, in boxes 23–26 on your answer sheet.*

23   Home medical aids

24   Regular amounts of exercise

25   Feelings of control over life

26   Feelings of loneliness

A	may cause heart disease.
B	can be helped by hormone treatment.
C	may cause rises in levels of stress hormones.
D	have cost the United States government more than $200 billion.
E	may help prevent mental decline.
F	may get stronger at night.
G	allow old people to be more independent.
H	can reduce stress in difficult situations.

READING PASSAGE 3

*You should spend about 20 minutes on **Questions 27–40**, which are based on Reading Passage 3 below.*

Numeration

One of the first great intellectual feats of a young child is learning how to talk, closely followed by learning how to count. From earliest childhood we are so bound up with our system of numeration that it is a feat of imagination to consider the problems faced by early humans who had not yet developed this facility. Careful consideration of our system of numeration leads to the conviction that, rather than being a facility that comes naturally to a person, it is one of the great and remarkable achievements of the human race.

It is impossible to learn the sequence of events that led to our developing the concept of number. Even the earliest of tribes had a system of numeration that, if not advanced, was sufficient for the tasks that they had to perform. Our ancestors had little use for actual numbers; instead their considerations would have been more of the kind *Is this enough?* rather than *How many?* when they were engaged in food gathering, for example. However, when early humans first began to reflect on the nature of things around them, they discovered that they needed an idea of number simply to keep their thoughts in order. As they began to settle, grow plants and herd animals, the need for a sophisticated number system became paramount. It will never be known how and when this numeration ability developed, but it is certain that numeration was well developed by the time humans had formed even semi-permanent settlements.

Evidence of early stages of arithmetic and numeration can be readily found. The indigenous peoples of Tasmania were only able to count *one, two, many*; those of South Africa counted *one, two, two and one, two twos, two twos and one,* and so on. But in real situations the number and words are often accompanied by gestures to help resolve any confusion. For example, when using the *one, two, many* type of system, the word *many* would mean, *Look at my hands and see how many fingers I am showing you.* This basic approach is limited in the range of numbers that it can express, but this range will generally suffice when dealing with the simpler aspects of human existence.

The lack of ability of some cultures to deal with large numbers is not really surprising. European languages, when traced back to their earlier version, are very poor in number words and expressions. The ancient Gothic word for ten, *tachund*, is used to express the number 100 as *tachund tachund*. By the seventh century, the word *teon* had become interchangeable with the *tachund* or *hund* of the Anglo-Saxon language, and so 100 was denoted as *hund teontig*, or ten times ten. The average person in the seventh century in Europe was not as familiar with numbers as we are today. In fact, to qualify as a witness in a court of law a man had to be able to count to nine!

Perhaps the most fundamental step in developing a sense of number is not the ability to count, but rather to see that a number is really an abstract idea instead of a simple attachment to a group of particular objects. It must have been within the grasp of the earliest humans to conceive that four birds are distinct from two birds; however, it is not an elementary step to associate the number 4, as connected with four birds, to the number 4, as connected with four rocks. Associating a number as one of the qualities of a specific object is a great hindrance to the development of a true number sense. When the number 4 can be registered in the mind as a specific word, independent of the object being referenced, the individual is ready to take the first step toward the development of a notational system for numbers and, from there, to arithmetic.

Traces of the very first stages in the development of numeration can be seen in several living languages today. The numeration system of the Tsimshian language in British Columbia contains seven distinct sets of words for numbers according to the class of the item being counted: for counting flat objects and animals, for round objects and time, for people, for long objects and trees, for canoes, for measures, and for counting when no particular object is being numerated. It seems that the last is a later development while the first six groups show the relics of an older system. This diversity of number names can also be found in some widely used languages such as Japanese.

Intermixed with the development of a number sense is the development of an ability to count. Counting is not directly related to the formation of a number concept because it is possible to count by matching the items being counted against a group of pebbles, grains of corn, or the counter's fingers. These aids would have been indispensable to very early people who would have found the process impossible without some form of mechanical aid. Such aids, while different, are still used even by the most educated in today's society due to their convenience. All counting ultimately involves reference to something other than the things being counted. At first it may have been grains or pebbles but now it is a memorised sequence of words that happen to be the names of the numbers.

Questions 27–31

*Complete each sentence with the correct ending, **A–G**, below.*

*Write the correct letter, **A–G**, in boxes 27–31 on your answer sheet.*

27   A developed system of numbering

28   An additional hand signal

29   In seventh-century Europe, the ability to count to a certain number

30   Thinking about numbers as concepts separate from physical objects

31   Expressing number differently according to class of item

A	was necessary in order to fulfil a civic role.
B	was necessary when people began farming.
C	was necessary for the development of arithmetic.
D	persists in all societies.
E	was used when the range of number words was restricted.
F	can be traced back to early European languages.
G	was a characteristic of early numeration systems.

Questions 32–40

Do the following statements agree with the information given in Reading Passage 3?

In boxes 32–40 on your answer sheet, write

TRUE	*if the statement agrees with the information*
FALSE	*if the statement contradicts the information*
NOT GIVEN	*if there is no information on this*

32   For the earliest tribes, the concept of sufficiency was more important than the concept of quantity.

33   Indigenous Tasmanians used only four terms to indicate numbers of objects.

34   Some peoples with simple number systems use body language to prevent misunderstanding of expressions of number.

35   All cultures have been able to express large numbers clearly.

36   The word 'thousand' has Anglo-Saxon origins.

37   In general, people in seventh-century Europe had poor counting ability.

38   In the Tsimshian language, the number for long objects and canoes is expressed with the same word.

39   The Tsimshian language contains both older and newer systems of counting.

40   Early peoples found it easier to count by using their fingers rather than a group of pebbles.

WRITING

WRITING TASK 1

You should spend about 20 minutes on this task.

> *The table below gives information about changes in modes of travel in England between 1985 and 2000.*
>
> *Summarise the information by selecting and reporting the main features, and make comparisons where relevant.*

Write at least 150 words.

Average distance in miles travelled per person per year, by mode of travel

	1985	2000
Walking	255	237
Bicycle	51	41
Car	3,199	4,806
Local bus	429	274
Long distance bus	54	124
Train	289	366
Taxi	13	42
Other	450	585
All modes	**4,740**	**6,475**

WRITING TASK 2

You should spend about 40 minutes on this task.

Write about the following topic:

> ***Successful sports professionals can earn a great deal more money than people in other important professions. Some people think this is fully justified while others think it is unfair.***
>
> ***Discuss both these views and give your own opinion.***

Give reasons for your answer and include any relevant examples from your own knowledge or experience.

Write at least 250 words.

SPEAKING

PART 1

The examiner asks the candidate about him/herself, his/her home, work or studies and other familiar topics.

EXAMPLE

Musical instruments

- Which instrument do you like listening to most? [Why?]
- Have you ever learned to play a musical instrument? [Which one?]
- Do you think children should learn to play a musical instrument at school? [Why/Why not?]
- How easy would it be to learn to play an instrument without a teacher? [Why?]

PART 2

Describe something healthy you enjoy doing.
You should say:
what you do
where you do it
who you do it with
and explain why you think doing this is healthy.

You will have to talk about the topic for one to two minutes.
You have one minute to think about what you are going to say.
You can make some notes to help you if you wish.

PART 3

Discussion topics:

Keeping fit and healthy

Example questions:
What do most people do to keep fit in your country?
How important is it for people to do some regular physical exercise?

Health and modern lifestyles

Example questions:
Why do some people think that modern lifestyles are not healthy?
Why do some people choose to lead unhealthy lives?
Should individuals or governments be responsible for making people's lifestyle healthy?
What could be done to encourage people to live in a healthy way?

Test 3

LISTENING

SECTION 1   *Questions 1–10*

Complete the form below.

*Write **ONE WORD AND/OR A NUMBER** for each answer.*

OPENING A BANK ACCOUNT

Example	*Answer*
Application for a	**_Current_** bank account

Type of current account: The **1** '.........................' account

Full name of applicant: Pieter Henes

Date of birth: **2** ....

Joint account holder(s):   No

Current address: **3** .... Exeter

Time at current address: **4** ....

Previous address: Rielsdorf 2, Utrecht, Holland

Telephone: **work 5** ....

                            home 796431

Occupation:	**6** ....
Identity (security):	Name of his **7** .... : Siti
Opening sum:	**8** € .... to be transferred from Fransen Bank, Utrecht
Statements:	Every **9** ....
Requests:	Supply information about the bank's **10** .... service

SECTION 2   *Questions 11–20*

Questions 11–13

*Choose the correct letter, **A**, **B** or **C**.*

THE HISTORY OF ROSEWOOD HOUSE

11 When the writer Sebastian George first saw Rosewood House, he

    A   thought he might rent it.
    B   felt it was too expensive for him.
    C   was unsure whether to buy it.

12 Before buying the house, George had

    A   experienced severe family problems.
    B   struggled to become a successful author.
    C   suffered a serious illness.

13 According to the speaker, George viewed Rosewood House as

    A   a rich source of material for his books.
    B   a way to escape from his work.
    C   a typical building of the region.

Questions 14–17

Label the map below.

*Write the correct letter, **A–J**, next to questions 14–17.*

ROSEWOOD HOUSE AND GARDENS

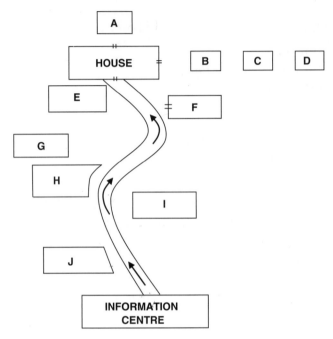

14	Pear Alley	....
15	Mulberry Garden	....
16	Shop	....
17	Tea Room	....

Questions 18–20

Complete the sentences below.

*Write **ONE WORD ONLY** for each answer.*

RIVER WALK

18 You can walk through the .... that goes along the river bank.

19 You can go over the .... and then into a wooded area.

20 On your way back, you could also go up to the ....

SECTION 3   *Questions 21–30*

Questions 21–24

Complete the sentences below.

*Write **NO MORE THAN THREE WORDS AND/OR A NUMBER** for each answer.*

MARKETING ASSIGNMENT

21 For their assignment, the students must investigate one part of the ....

22 The method the students must use to collect data is ....

23 In total, the students must interview .... people.

24 Jack thinks the music preferences of .... listeners are similar.

Questions 25–30

Complete the notes below.

*Write **NO MORE THAN TWO WORDS** for each answer.*

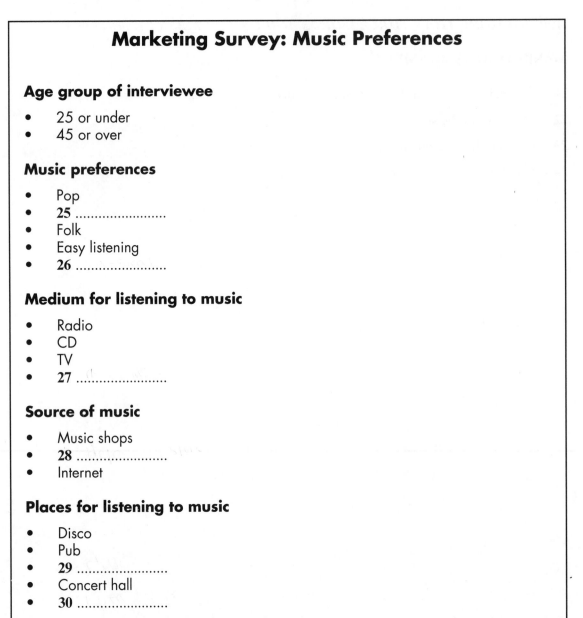

Marketing Survey: Music Preferences

Age group of interviewee

- 25 or under
- 45 or over

Music preferences

- Pop
- **25** ....
- Folk
- Easy listening
- **26** ....

Medium for listening to music

- Radio
- CD
- TV
- **27** ....

Source of music

- Music shops
- **28** ....
- Internet

Places for listening to music

- Disco
- Pub
- **29** ....
- Concert hall
- **30** ....

SECTION 4   *Questions 31–40*

Questions 31–34

Choose the correct letter, A, B or C.

IRELAND IN THE NEOLITHIC PERIOD

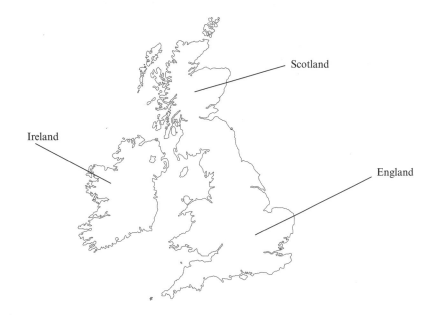

31   According to the speaker, it is not clear

   A   when the farming economy was introduced to Ireland.
   B   why people began to farm in Ireland.
   C   where the early Irish farmers came from.

32   What point does the speaker make about breeding animals in Neolithic Ireland?

   A   Their numbers must have been above a certain level.
   B   They were under threat from wild animals.
   C   Some species died out during this period.

33   What does the speaker say about the transportation of animals?

   A   Livestock would have limited the distance the farmers could sail.
   B   Neolithic boats were too primitive to have been used.
   C   Probably only a few breeding animals were imported.

34   What is the main evidence for cereal crops in Neolithic Ireland?

   A   the remains of burnt grain in pots
   B   the marks left on pots by grains
   C   the patterns painted on the surface of pots

Questions 35–40

Complete the sentences below.

*Write **NO MORE THAN TWO WORDS** for each answer.*

STONE TOOLS

35   Ploughs could either have been pulled by .... or by cattle.

•   The farmers needed homes which were permanent dwellings.

36   In the final stages of axe-making, ... and .... were necessary for grinding and polishing.

37   Irish axes were exported from Ireland to .... and England.

POTTERY MAKING

•   The colonisers used clay to make pots.

38   The .... of the pots was often polished to make them watertight.

39   Clay from .... areas was generally used.

40   Decoration was only put around the .... of the earliest pots.

READING

READING PASSAGE 1

*You should spend about 20 minutes on **Questions 1–13**, which are based on Reading Passage 1 below.*

A The Lumière Brothers opened their Cinematographe, at 14 Boulevard des Capucines in Paris, to 100 paying customers over 100 years ago, on December 8, 1895. Before the eyes of the stunned, thrilled audience, photographs came to life and moved across a flat screen.

B So ordinary and routine has this become to us that it takes a determined leap of the imagination to grasp the impact of those first moving images. But it is worth trying, for to understand the initial shock of those images is to understand the extraordinary power and magic of cinema, the unique, hypnotic quality that has made film the most dynamic, effective art form of the 20th century.

C One of the Lumière Brothers' earliest films was a 30-second piece which showed a section of a railway platform flooded with sunshine. A train appears and heads straight for the camera. And that is all that happens. Yet the Russian director Andrei Tarkovsky, one of the greatest of all film artists, described the film as a 'work of genius'. 'As the train approached,' wrote Tarkovsky, 'panic started in the theatre: people jumped and ran away. That was the moment when cinema was born. The frightened audience could not accept that they were watching a mere picture. Pictures were still, only reality moved; this must, therefore, be reality. In their confusion, they feared that a real train was about to crush them.'

D Early cinema audiences often experienced the same confusion. In time, the idea of film became familiar, the magic was accepted – but it never stopped being magic. Film has never lost its unique power to embrace its audiences and transport them to a different world. For Tarkovsky, the key to that magic was the way in which cinema created a dynamic image of the real flow of events. A still picture could only imply the existence of time, while time in a novel passed at the whim of the reader. But in cinema, the real, objective flow of time was captured.

E One effect of this realism was to educate the world about itself. For cinema makes the world smaller. Long before people travelled to America or anywhere else, they knew what other places looked like; they knew how other people worked and lived. Overwhelmingly, the lives recorded – at least in film fiction – have been American. From the earliest days of the industry, Hollywood has dominated the world film market. American imagery – the cars, the cities, the cowboys – became the primary imagery of film. Film carried American life and values around the globe.

F And, thanks to film, future generations will know the 20th century more intimately than any other period. We can only imagine what life was like in the 14th century or in classical Greece. But the life of the modern world has been recorded on film in massive, encyclopaedic detail. We shall be known better than any preceding generations.

G The 'star' was another natural consequence of cinema. The cinema star was effectively born in 1910. Film personalities have such an immediate presence that, inevitably, they become super-real. Because we watch them so closely and because everybody in the world seems to know who they are, they appear more real to us than we do ourselves. The star as magnified human self is one of cinema's most strange and enduring legacies.

H   Cinema has also given a new lease of life to the idea of the story. When the Lumière Brothers and other pioneers began showing off this new invention, it was by no means obvious how it would be used. All that mattered at first was the wonder of movement. Indeed, some said that, once this novelty had worn off, cinema would fade away. It was no more than a passing gimmick, a fairground attraction.

I   Cinema might, for example, have become primarily a documentary form. Or it might

have developed like television – as a strange, noisy transfer of music, information and narrative. But what happened was that it became, overwhelmingly, a medium for telling stories. Originally these were conceived as short stories – early producers doubted the ability of audiences to concentrate for more than the length of a reel. Then, in 1912, an Italian 2-hour film was hugely successful, and Hollywood settled upon the novel-length narrative that remains the dominant cinematic convention of today.

J   And it has all happened so quickly. Almost unbelievably, it is a mere 100 years since that train arrived and the audience screamed and fled, convinced by the dangerous reality of what they saw, and, perhaps, suddenly aware that the world could never be the same again – that, maybe, it could be better, brighter, more astonishing, more real than reality.

Questions 1–5

Reading Passage 1 has ten paragraphs, **A–J**.

Which paragraph contains the following information?

*Write the correct letter, **A–J**, in boxes 1–5 on your answer sheet.*

1   the location of the first cinema

2   how cinema came to focus on stories

3   the speed with which cinema has changed

4   how cinema teaches us about other cultures

5   the attraction of actors in films

Questions 6–9

Do the following statements agree with the views of the writer in Reading Passage 1?

In boxes 6–9 on your answer sheet, write

YES	*if the statement agrees with the views of the writer*
NO	*if the statement contradicts the views of the writer*
NOT GIVEN	*if it is impossible to say what the writer thinks about this*

6   It is important to understand how the first audiences reacted to the cinema.

7   The Lumière Brothers' film about the train was one of the greatest films ever made.

8   Cinema presents a biased view of other countries.

9   Storylines were important in very early cinema.

Questions 10–13

*Choose the correct letter, **A**, **B**, **C** or **D**.*

Write the correct letter in boxes 10–13 on your answer sheet.

10 The writer refers to the film of the train in order to demonstrate

  A the simplicity of early films.
  B the impact of early films.
  C how short early films were.
  D how imaginative early films were.

11 In Tarkovsky's opinion, the attraction of the cinema is that it

  A aims to impress its audience.
  B tells stories better than books.
  C illustrates the passing of time.
  D describes familiar events.

12 When cinema first began, people thought that

  A it would always tell stories.
  B it should be used in fairgrounds.
  C its audiences were unappreciative.
  D its future was uncertain.

13 What is the best title for this passage?

  A The rise of the cinema star
  B Cinema and novels compared
  C The domination of Hollywood
  D The power of the big screen

READING PASSAGE 2

*You should spend about 20 minutes on **Questions 14–27**, which are based on Reading Passage 2 on the following pages.*

Questions 14–18

Reading Passage 2 contains six Key Points.

*Choose the correct heading for Key Points **TWO** to **SIX** from the list of headings below.*

*Write the correct number, **i–viii**, in boxes 14–18 on your answer sheet.*

List of Headings
i   Ensure the reward system is fair
ii   Match rewards to individuals
iii   Ensure targets are realistic
iv   Link rewards to achievement
v   Encourage managers to take more responsibility
vi   Recognise changes in employees' performance over time
vii   Establish targets and give feedback
viii   Ensure employees are suited to their jobs

Example	*Answer*
Key Point **One**	**viii**

14   Key Point **Two**

15   Key Point **Three**

16   Key Point **Four**

17   Key Point **Five**

18   Key Point **Six**

Motivating Employees under Adverse Conditions

THE CHALLENGE

It is a great deal easier to motivate employees in a growing organisation than a declining one. When organisations are expanding and adding personnel, promotional opportunities, pay rises, and the excitement of being associated with a dynamic organisation create feelings of optimism. Management is able to use the growth to entice and encourage employees. When an organisation is shrinking, the best and most mobile workers are prone to leave voluntarily. Unfortunately, they are the ones the organisation can least afford to lose – those with the highest skills and experience. The minor employees remain because their job options are limited.

Morale also suffers during decline. People fear they may be the next to be made redundant. Productivity often suffers, as employees spend their time sharing rumours and providing one another with moral support rather than focusing on their jobs. For those whose jobs are secure, pay increases are rarely possible. Pay cuts, unheard of during times of growth, may even be imposed. The challenge to management is how to motivate employees under such retrenchment conditions. The ways of meeting this challenge can be broadly divided into six Key Points, which are outlined below.

KEY POINT ONE

There is an abundance of evidence to support the motivational benefits that result from carefully matching people to jobs. For example, if the job is running a small business or an autonomous unit within a larger business, high achievers should be sought. However, if the job to be filled is a managerial post in a large bureaucratic organisation, a candidate who has a high need for power and a low need for affiliation should be selected. Accordingly, high achievers should not be put into jobs that are inconsistent with their needs. High achievers will do best when the job provides moderately challenging goals and where there is independence and feedback. However, it should be remembered that not everybody is motivated by jobs that are high in independence, variety and responsibility.

KEY POINT TWO

The literature on goal-setting theory suggests that managers should ensure that all employees have specific goals and receive comments on how well they are doing in those goals. For those with high achievement needs, typically a minority in any organisation, the existence of external goals is less important because high achievers are already internally motivated. The next factor to be determined is whether the goals should be assigned by a manager or collectively set in conjunction with the employees. The answer to that depends on perceptions of goal acceptance and the organisation's culture. If resistance to goals is expected, the use of participation in goal-setting should increase acceptance. If participation is inconsistent with the culture, however, goals should be assigned. If participation and the culture are incongruous, employees are likely to perceive the participation process as manipulative and be negatively affected by it.

KEY POINT THREE
Regardless of whether goals are achievable or well within management's perceptions of the employee's ability, if employees see them as unachievable they will reduce their effort. Managers must be sure, therefore, that employees feel confident that their efforts *can* lead to performance goals. For managers, this means that employees must have the capability of doing the job and must regard the appraisal process as valid.

KEY POINT FOUR
Since employees have different needs, what acts as a reinforcement for one may not for another. Managers could use their knowledge of each employee to personalise the rewards over which they have control. Some of the more obvious rewards that managers allocate include pay, promotions, autonomy, job scope and depth, and the opportunity to participate in goal-setting and decision-making.

KEY POINT FIVE
Managers need to make rewards contingent on performance. To reward factors other than performance will only reinforce those other factors. Key rewards such as pay increases and promotions or advancements should be allocated for the attainment of the employee's specific goals. Consistent with maximising the impact of rewards, managers should look for ways to increase their visibility. Eliminating the secrecy surrounding pay by openly communicating everyone's remuneration, publicising performance bonuses and allocating annual salary increases in a lump sum rather than spreading them out over an entire year are examples of actions that will make rewards more visible and potentially more motivating.

KEY POINT SIX
The way rewards are distributed should be transparent so that employees perceive that rewards or outcomes are equitable and equal to the inputs given. On a simplistic level, experience, abilities, effort and other obvious inputs should explain differences in pay, responsibility and other obvious outcomes. The problem, however, is complicated by the existence of dozens of inputs and outcomes and by the fact that employee groups place different degrees of importance on them. For instance, a study comparing clerical and production workers identified nearly twenty inputs and outcomes. The clerical workers considered factors such as quality of work performed and job knowledge near the top of their list, but these were at the bottom of the production workers' list. Similarly, production workers thought that the most important inputs were intelligence and personal involvement with task accomplishment, two factors that were quite low in the importance ratings of the clerks. There were also important, though less dramatic, differences on the outcome side. For example, production workers rated advancement very highly, whereas clerical workers rated advancement in the lower third of their list. Such findings suggest that one person's equity is another's inequity, so an ideal should probably weigh different inputs and outcomes according to employee group.

Questions 19–24

Do the following statements agree with the views of the writer in Reading Passage 2?

In boxes 19–24 on your answer sheet, write

> **YES**   *if the statement agrees with the views of the writer*
> **NO**   *if the statement contradicts the views of the writer*
> **NOT GIVEN**   *if it is impossible to say what the writer thinks about this*

19   A shrinking organisation tends to lose its less skilled employees rather than its more skilled employees.

20   It is easier to manage a small business than a large business.

21   High achievers are well suited to team work.

22   Some employees can feel manipulated when asked to participate in goal-setting.

23   The staff appraisal process should be designed by employees.

24   Employees' earnings should be disclosed to everyone within the organisation.

Questions 25–27

Look at the following groups of workers (Questions 25–27) and the list of descriptions below.

Match each group with the correct description, A–E.

Write the correct letter, A–E, in boxes 25–27 on your answer sheet.

25   high achievers

26   clerical workers

27   production workers

List of Descriptions

A   They judge promotion to be important.
B   They have less need of external goals.
C   They think that the quality of their work is important.
D   They resist goals which are imposed.
E   They have limited job options.

READING PASSAGE 3

*You should spend about 20 minutes on **Questions 28–40**, which are based on Reading Passage 3 below.*

The Search for the Anti-aging Pill

In government laboratories and elsewhere, scientists are seeking a drug able to prolong life and youthful vigor. Studies of caloric restriction are showing the way

As researchers on aging noted recently, no treatment on the market today has been proved to slow human aging – the build-up of molecular and cellular damage that increases vulnerability to infirmity as we grow older. But one intervention, consumption of a low-calorie* yet nutritionally balanced diet, works incredibly well in a broad range of animals, increasing longevity and prolonging good health. Those findings suggest that caloric restriction could delay aging and increase longevity in humans, too.

Unfortunately, for maximum benefit, people would probably have to reduce their caloric intake by roughly thirty per cent, equivalent to dropping from 2,500 calories a day to 1,750. Few mortals could stick to that harsh a regimen, especially for years on end. But what if someone could create a pill that mimicked the physiological effects of eating less without actually forcing people to eat less? Could such a 'caloric-restriction mimetic', as we call it, enable people to stay healthy longer, postponing age-related disorders (such as diabetes, arteriosclerosis, heart disease and cancer) until very late in life? Scientists first posed this question in the mid-1990s, after researchers came upon a chemical agent that in rodents seemed to reproduce many of caloric restriction's benefits. No compound that would safely achieve the same feat in people has been found yet, but the search has been informative and has fanned hope that caloric-restriction (CR) mimetics can indeed be developed eventually.

The benefits of caloric restriction

The hunt for CR mimetics grew out of a desire to better understand caloric restriction's many effects on the body. Scientists first recognized the value of the practice more than 60 years ago, when they found that rats fed a low-calorie diet lived longer on average than free-feeding rats and also had a reduced incidence of conditions that become increasingly common in old age. What is more, some of the treated animals survived longer than the oldest-living animals in the control group, which means that the maximum lifespan (the oldest attainable age), not merely the normal lifespan, increased. Various interventions, such as infection-fighting drugs, can increase a population's average survival time, but only approaches that slow the body's rate of aging will increase the maximum lifespan.

The rat findings have been replicated many times and extended to creatures ranging from yeast to fruit flies, worms, fish, spiders, mice and hamsters. Until fairly recently, the studies were limited to short-lived creatures genetically distant from humans. But caloric-restriction projects underway in two species more closely related to humans – rhesus and squirrel monkeys – have made scientists optimistic that CR mimetics could help people.

---

* *calorie:* a measure of the energy value of food

The monkey projects demonstrate that, compared with control animals that eat normally, caloric-restricted monkeys have lower body temperatures and levels of the pancreatic hormone insulin, and they retain more youthful levels of certain hormones that tend to fall with age.

The caloric-restricted animals also look better on indicators of risk for age-related diseases. For example, they have lower blood pressure and triglyceride levels (signifying a decreased likelihood of heart disease), and they have more normal blood glucose levels (pointing to a reduced risk for diabetes, which is marked by unusually high blood glucose levels). Further, it has recently been shown that rhesus monkeys kept on caloric-restricted diets for an extended time (nearly 15 years) have less chronic disease. They and the other monkeys must be followed still longer, however, to know whether low-calorie intake can increase both average and maximum lifespans in monkeys. Unlike the multitude of elixirs being touted as the latest anti-aging cure, CR mimetics would alter fundamental processes that underlie aging. We aim to develop compounds that fool cells into activating maintenance and repair.

How a prototype caloric-restriction mimetic works

The best-studied candidate for a caloric-restriction mimetic, 2DG (2-deoxy-D-glucose), works by interfering with the way cells process glucose. It has proved toxic at some doses in animals and so cannot be used in humans. But it has demonstrated that chemicals can replicate the effects of caloric restriction; the trick is finding the right one.

Cells use the glucose from food to generate ATP (adenosine triphosphate), the molecule that powers many activities in the body. By limiting food intake, caloric restriction minimizes the amount of glucose entering cells and decreases ATP generation. When 2DG is administered to animals that eat normally, glucose reaches cells in abundance but the drug prevents most of it from being processed and thus reduces ATP synthesis. Researchers have proposed several explanations for why interruption of glucose processing and ATP production might retard aging. One possibility relates to the ATP-making machinery's emission of free radicals, which are thought to contribute to aging and to such age-related diseases as cancer by damaging cells. Reduced operation of the machinery should limit their production and thereby constrain the damage. Another hypothesis suggests that decreased processing of glucose could indicate to cells that food is scarce (even if it isn't) and induce them to shift into an anti-aging mode that emphasizes preservation of the organism over such 'luxuries' as growth and reproduction.

Questions 28–32

Do the following statements agree with the claims of the writer in Reading Passage 3?

In boxes 28–32 on your answer sheet, write

YES   *if the statement agrees with the claims of the writer*
NO   *if the statement contradicts the claims of the writer*
NOT GIVEN   *if it is impossible to say what the writer thinks about this*

28   Studies show drugs available today can delay the process of growing old.

29   There is scientific evidence that eating fewer calories may extend human life.

30   Not many people are likely to find a caloric-restricted diet attractive.

31   Diet-related diseases are common in older people.

32   In experiments, rats who ate what they wanted led shorter lives than rats on a low-calorie diet.

Questions 33–37

Classify the following descriptions as relating to

A   *caloric-restricted monkeys*
B   *control monkeys*
C   *neither caloric-restricted monkeys nor control monkeys*

*Write the correct letter, **A**, **B** or **C**, in boxes 33–37 on your answer sheet.*

33   Monkeys were less likely to become diabetic.

34   Monkeys experienced more chronic disease.

35   Monkeys have been shown to experience a longer than average life span.

36   Monkeys enjoyed a reduced chance of heart disease.

37   Monkeys produced greater quantities of insulin.

Questions 38–40

Complete the flow-chart below.

*Choose **NO MORE THAN TWO WORDS** from the passage for each answer.*

Write your answers in boxes 38–40 on your answer sheet.

How a caloric-restriction mimetic works

CR mimetic

↓

less **38** .... is processed

↓

production of ATP is decreased

↙   ↘

Theory 1:

cells less damaged by disease because
fewer **39** .... are emitted

Theory 2:

cells focus on **40** ....
because food is in short supply

WRITING

WRITING TASK 1

You should spend about 20 minutes on this task.

> **The diagrams below show the life cycle of the silkworm and the stages in the production of silk cloth.**
>
> **Summarise the information by selecting and reporting the main features, and make comparisons where relevant.**

Write at least 150 words.

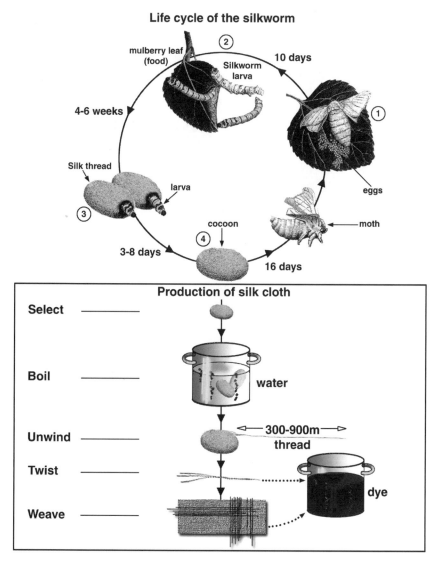

Life cycle of the silkworm

Production of silk cloth

WRITING TASK 2

You should spend about 40 minutes on this task.

Write about the following topic:

> *Some people believe that visitors to other countries should follow local customs and behaviour. Others disagree and think that the host country should welcome cultural differences.*
>
> *Discuss both these views and give your own opinion.*

Give reasons for your answer and include any relevant examples from your own knowledge or experience.

Write at least 250 words.

SPEAKING

PART 1

The examiner asks the candidate about him/herself, his/her home, work or studies and other familiar topics.

EXAMPLE

Traffic where you live

- How do most people travel to work where you live?
- What traffic problems are there in your area? [Why?]
- How do traffic problems affect you?
- How would you reduce the traffic problems in your area?

PART 2

> **Describe a game or sport you enjoy playing.**
>
> **You should say:**
>   **what kind of game or sport it is**
>   **who you play it with**
>   **where you play it**
> **and explain why you enjoy playing it.**

You will have to talk about the topic for one to two minutes.
You have one minute to think about what you are going to say.
You can make some notes to help you if you wish.

PART 3

Discussion topics:

Children's games

Example questions:

How have games changed from the time when you were a child?
Do you think this has been a positive change? Why?
Why do you think children like playing games?

Games and competition

Example questions:

Do you think competitive games are good or bad for children? In what ways?
How can games sometimes help to unite people?
Why is competition often seen as important in today's society?

Test 4

SECTION 1   Questions 1–10

Complete the notes below.

*Write **NO MORE THAN TWO WORDS AND/OR A NUMBER** for each answer.*

Example	*Answer*
Title of conference:	***Future Directions*** in Computing

Three day cost: 1 £ ....
Payment by **2** .... or on arrival

Accommodation:

Conference Centre

- 3 £ .... per night
- near to conference rooms

Guest House

- 4 £ .... per night
- approximately **5** .... walk from Conference Centre

Further documents to be sent:

- 6 ....
- an application form

Location:

Conference Centre is on 7 .... Park Road, next to the 8 ....

Taxi costs 9 £ .... or take bus number 10 .... from station.

SECTION 2   *Questions 11–20*

Questions 11–13

Which team will do each of the following jobs?

*Choose **THREE** answers from the box and write the correct letter, **A–D**, next to questions 11–13.*

	Teams
A	the blue team
B	the yellow team
C	the green team
D	the red team

11   checking entrance tickets ....

12   preparing refreshments ....

13   directing car-park traffic ....

Questions 14–20

Complete the table below.

Write **NO MORE THAN THREE WORDS AND/OR A NUMBER** *for each answer.*

Travel Expo Temporary Staff Orientation Programme		
Time	**Event**	**Details**
9.30 am	Talk by Anne Smith	• information about pay • will give out the **14** .... forms
10.00 am	Talk by Peter Chen	• will discuss Conference Centre plan • will explain about arrangements for **15** .... and fire exits
10.30 am	Coffee Break	• go to Staff Canteen on the **16** ....
11.00 am	Video Presentation	• go to **17** .... • video title: **18** ....
12.00	Buffet Lunch	• go to the **19** .... on 1st floor
1.00 pm	Meet the **20**	
3.00 pm	Finish	

SECTION 3   *Questions 21–30*

Questions 21–25

Complete the summary below.

Write ONE WORD ONLY for each answer.

The School of Education Libraries

The libraries on both sites provide internet access and have a variety of
21 .... materials on education.

The Castle Road library has books on sociology, together with 22 ....
and other resources relevant to the majority of 23 .... school subjects.

The Fordham library includes resources for teaching in 24 .... education
and special needs.

Current issues of periodicals are available at both libraries, although
25 .... issues are only available at Fordham.

Questions 26 and 27

Answer the questions below.

Write NO MORE THAN TWO WORDS AND/OR A NUMBER for each answer.

26   Which books cannot be renewed by telephone or email?

....

27   How much time is allowed to return recalled books?

....

Questions 28–30

*Choose **THREE** letters, A–G.*

Which **THREE** topics do this term's study skills workshops cover?

A	An introduction to the Internet
B	How to carry out research for a dissertation
C	Making good use of the whole range of library services
D	Planning a dissertation
E	Standard requirements when writing a dissertation
F	Using the Internet when doing research
G	What books and technical resources are available in the library

SECTION 4   *Questions 31–40*

Questions 31–34

Choose the correct letter, A, B or C.

31   When did Asiatic lions develop as a separate sub-species?

    A   about 10,000 years ago
    B   about 100,000 years ago
    C   about 1,000,000 years ago

32   Pictures of Asiatic lions can be seen on ancient coins from

    A   Greece.
    B   The Middle East.
    C   India.

33   Asiatic lions disappeared from Europe

    A   2,500 years ago.
    B   2,000 years ago.
    C   1,900 years ago.

34   Very few African lions have

    A   a long mane.
    B   a coat with varied colours.
    C   a fold of skin on their stomach.

Questions 35–40

Complete the sentences below.

Write **NO MORE THAN TWO WORDS AND/OR A NUMBER** *for each answer.*

THE GIR SANCTUARY

35   The sanctuary has an area of approximately .... square kilometres.

36   One threat to the lions in the sanctuary is ....

37   The ancestors of the Gir Sanctuary lions were protected by a ....

38   A large part of the lions' .... consists of animals belonging to local farmers.

39   The lions sometimes .... , especially when water is short.

40   In ancient India a man would fight a lion as a test of ....

READING

READING PASSAGE 1

*You should spend about 20 minutes on **Questions 1–13**, which are based on Reading Passage 1 on the following pages.*

Questions 1–7

Reading Passage 1 has seven paragraphs, **A–G**.

Choose the correct heading for each paragraph from the list of headings below.

*Write the correct number, **i–x**, in boxes 1–7 on your answer sheet.*

List of Headings

i	Not all doctors are persuaded
ii	Choosing the best offers
iii	Who is responsible for the increase in promotions?
iv	Fighting the drug companies
v	An example of what doctors expect from drug companies
vi	Gifts include financial incentives
vii	Research shows that promotion works
viii	The high costs of research
ix	The positive side of drugs promotion
x	Who really pays for doctors' free gifts?

---

1 Paragraph **A**

2 Paragraph **B**

3 Paragraph **C**

4 Paragraph **D**

5 Paragraph **E**

6 Paragraph **F**

7 Paragraph **G**

Doctoring sales

Pharmaceuticals is one of the most profitable industries in North America. But do the drugs industry's sales and marketing strategies go too far?

A   A few months ago Kim Schaefer, sales representative of a major global pharmaceutical company, walked into a medical center in New York to bring information and free samples of her company's latest products. That day she was lucky – a doctor was available to see her. 'The last rep offered me a trip to Florida. What do you have?' the physician asked. He was only half joking.

B   What was on offer that day was a pair of tickets for a New York musical. But on any given day, what Schaefer can offer is typical for today's drugs rep – a car trunk full of promotional gifts and gadgets, a budget that could buy lunches and dinners for a small country, hundreds of free drug samples and the freedom to give a physician $200 to prescribe her new product to the next six patients who fit the drug's profile. And she also has a few $1,000 honoraria to offer in exchange for doctors' attendance at her company's next educational lecture.

C   Selling pharmaceuticals is a daily exercise in ethical judgement. Salespeople like Schaefer walk the line between the common practice of buying a prospect's time with a free meal, and bribing doctors to prescribe their drugs. They work in an industry highly criticized for its sales and marketing practices, but find themselves in the middle of the age-old chicken-or-egg question – businesses won't use strategies that don't work, so are doctors to blame for the escalating extravagance of pharmaceutical marketing? Or is it the industry's responsibility to decide the boundaries?

D   The explosion in the sheer number of salespeople in the field – and the amount of funding used to promote their causes – forces close examination of the pressures, influences and relationships between drug reps and doctors. Salespeople provide much-needed information and education to physicians. In many cases the glossy brochures, article reprints and prescriptions they deliver are primary sources of drug education for healthcare givers. With the huge investment the industry has placed in face-to-face selling, salespeople have essentially become specialists in one drug or group of drugs – a tremendous advantage in getting the attention of busy doctors in need of quick information.

E   But the sales push rarely stops in the office. The flashy brochures and pamphlets left by the sales reps are often followed up with meals at expensive restaurants, meetings in warm and sunny places, and an inundation of promotional gadgets. Rarely do patients watch a doctor write with a pen that isn't emblazoned with a drug's name, or see a nurse use a tablet not bearing a pharmaceutical company's logo. Millions of dollars are spent by pharmaceutical companies on promotional products like coffee mugs, shirts, umbrellas, and golf balls. Money well spent? It's hard to tell. 'I've been the recipient of golf balls from one company and I use them, but it doesn't make me prescribe their medicine,' says one doctor. 'I tend to think I'm not influenced by what they give me.'

F   Free samples of new and expensive drugs might be the single most effective way of getting doctors and patients to become loyal to a product. Salespeople hand out hundreds of dollars' worth of samples each week – $7.2 billion worth of them in one year. Though few comprehensive studies have been conducted, one by the University of Washington investigated how drug sample availability affected what physicians prescribe. A total of 131 doctors self-reported their prescribing patterns – the conclusion was that the availability of samples led them to dispense and prescribe drugs that differed from their preferred drug choice.

G   The bottom line is that pharmaceutical companies as a whole invest more in marketing than they do in research and development. And patients are the ones who pay – in the form of sky-rocketing prescription prices – for every pen that's handed out, every free theatre ticket, and every steak dinner eaten. In the end the fact remains that pharmaceutical companies have every right to make a profit and will continue to find new ways to increase sales. But as the medical world continues to grapple with what's acceptable and what's not, it is clear that companies must continue to be heavily scrutinized for their sales and marketing strategies.

Questions 8–13

Do the following statements agree with the views of the writer in Reading Passage 1?

In boxes 8–13 on your answer sheet, write

> **YES**   *if the statement agrees with the views of the writer*
> **NO**   *if the statement contradicts the views of the writer*
> **NOT GIVEN**   *if it is impossible to say what the writer thinks about this*

8   Sales representatives like Kim Schaefer work to a very limited budget.

9   Kim Schaefer's marketing technique may be open to criticism on moral grounds.

10   The information provided by drug companies is of little use to doctors.

11   Evidence of drug promotion is clearly visible in the healthcare environment.

12   The drug companies may give free drug samples to patients without doctors' prescriptions.

13   It is legitimate for drug companies to make money.

READING PASSAGE 2

*You should spend about 20 minutes on **Questions 14–26**, which are based on Reading Passage 2 below.*

Do literate women make better mothers?

Children in developing countries are healthier and more likely to survive past the age of five when their mothers can read and write. Experts in public health accepted this idea decades ago, but until now no one has been able to show that a woman's ability to read in itself improves her children's chances of survival.

Most literate women learnt to read in primary school, and the fact that a woman has had an education may simply indicate her family's wealth or that it values its children more highly. Now a long-term study carried out in Nicaragua has eliminated these factors by showing that teaching reading to poor adult women, who would otherwise have remained illiterate, has a direct effect on their children's health and survival.

In 1979, the government of Nicaragua established a number of social programmes, including a National Literacy Crusade. By 1985, about 300,000 illiterate adults from all over the country, many of whom had never attended primary school, had learnt how to read, write and use numbers.

During this period, researchers from the Liverpool School of Tropical Medicine, the Central American Institute of Health in Nicaragua, the National Autonomous University of Nicaragua and the Costa Rican Institute of Health interviewed nearly 3,000 women, some of whom had learnt to read as children, some during the literacy crusade and some who had never learnt at all. The women were asked how many children they had given birth to and how many of them had died in infancy. The research teams also examined the surviving children to find out how well-nourished they were.

The investigators' findings were striking. In the late 1970s, the infant mortality rate for the children of illiterate mothers was around 110 deaths per thousand live births. At this point in their lives, those mothers who later went on to learn to read had a similar level of child mortality (105/1000). For women educated in primary school, however, the infant mortality rate was significantly lower, at 80 per thousand.

In 1985, after the National Literacy Crusade had ended, the infant mortality figures for those who remained illiterate and for those educated in primary school remained more or less unchanged. For those women who learnt to read through the campaign, the infant mortality rate was 84 per thousand, an impressive 21 points lower than for those women who were still illiterate. The children of the newly-literate mothers were also better nourished than those of women who could not read.

Why are the children of literate mothers better off? According to Peter Sandiford of the Liverpool School of Tropical Medicine, no one knows for certain. Child health was not on the curriculum during the women's lessons, so he and his colleagues are looking at other factors. They are working with the same group of 3,000 women, to try to find out whether reading mothers make better use of hospitals and clinics, opt for smaller families, exert more control at home, learn modern childcare techniques more quickly, or whether they merely have more respect for themselves and their children.

The Nicaraguan study may have important implications for governments and aid agencies that need to know where to direct their resources. Sandiford says that there is increasing evidence that female education, at any age, is 'an important health intervention in its own right'. The results of the study lend support to the World Bank's recommendation that education budgets in developing countries should be increased, not just to help their economies, but also to improve child health.

'We've known for a long time that maternal education is important,' says John Cleland of the London School of Hygiene and Tropical Medicine. 'But we thought that even if we started educating girls today, we'd have to wait a generation for the pay-off. The Nicaraguan study suggests we may be able to bypass that.'

Cleland warns that the Nicaraguan crusade was special in many ways, and similar campaigns elsewhere might not work as well. It is notoriously difficult to teach adults skills that do not have an immediate impact on their everyday lives, and many literacy campaigns in other countries have been much less successful. 'The crusade was part of a larger effort to bring a better life to the people,' says Cleland. Replicating these conditions in other countries will be a major challenge for development workers.

Questions 14–18

Complete the summary using the list of words, A–J, below.

Write the correct letter, A–J, in boxes 14–18 on your answer sheet.

NB   You may use any letter more than once.

The Nicaraguan National Literacy Crusade aimed to teach large numbers of illiterate
14 .... to read and write. Public health experts have known for many years that
there is a connection between child health and **15** .... However, it has not
previously been known whether these two factors were directly linked or not. This question
has been investigated by **16** .... in Nicaragua. As a result, factors such as
17 .... and attitudes to children have been eliminated, and it has been shown
that **18** .... can in itself improve infant health and survival.

A child literacy   **B** men and women   **C** an international research team

D medical care   **E** mortality   **F** maternal literacy

G adults and children   **H** paternal literacy   **I** a National Literacy Crusade

J family wealth

Questions 19–24

Do the following statements agree with the claims of the writer in Reading Passage 2?

In boxes 19–24 on your answer sheet, write

> **YES** if the statement agrees with the claims of the writer
> **NO** if the statement contradicts the claims of the writer
> **NOT GIVEN** if it is impossible to say what the writer thinks about this

19 About a thousand of the women interviewed by the researchers had learnt to read when they were children.

20 Before the National Literacy Crusade, illiterate women had approximately the same levels of infant mortality as those who had learnt to read in primary school.

21 Before and after the National Literacy Crusade, the child mortality rate for the illiterate women stayed at about 110 deaths for each thousand live births.

22 The women who had learnt to read through the National Literacy Crusade showed the greatest change in infant mortality levels.

23 The women who had learnt to read through the National Literacy Crusade had the lowest rates of child mortality.

24 After the National Literacy Crusade, the children of the women who remained illiterate were found to be severely malnourished.

Questions 25 and 26

*Choose **TWO** letters, A–E.*

Write the correct letters in boxes 25 and 26 on your answer sheet.

Which **TWO** important implications drawn from the Nicaraguan study are mentioned by the writer of the passage?

    A It is better to educate mature women than young girls.

    B Similar campaigns in other countries would be equally successful.

    C The effects of maternal literacy programmes can be seen very quickly.

    D Improving child health can quickly affect a country's economy.

    E Money spent on female education will improve child health.

READING PASSAGE 3

*You should spend about 20 minutes on **Questions 27–40**, which are based on Reading Passage 3 on the following pages.*

Questions 27–30

Reading Passage 3 has six sections, **A–F**.

*Choose the correct heading for sections **A–D** from the list of headings below.*

*Write the correct number, **i–vii**, in boxes 27–30 on your answer sheet.*

List of Headings

i   The role of video violence

ii   The failure of government policy

iii   Reasons for the increased rate of bullying

iv   Research into how common bullying is in British schools

v   The reaction from schools to enquiries about bullying

vi   The effect of bullying on the children involved

vii   Developments that have led to a new approach by schools

---

27   Section **A**

28   Section **B**

29   Section **C**

30   Section **D**

Persistent bullying is one of the worst experiences a child can face. How can it be prevented? Peter Smith, Professor of Psychology at the University of Sheffield, directed the Sheffield Anti-Bullying Intervention Project, funded by the Department for Education. Here he reports on his findings.

A   Bullying can take a variety of forms, from the verbal – being taunted or called hurtful names – to the physical – being kicked or shoved – as well as indirect forms, such as being excluded from social groups. A survey I conducted with Irene Whitney found that in British primary schools up to a quarter of pupils reported experience of bullying, which in about one in ten cases was persistent. There was less bullying in secondary schools, with about one in twenty-five suffering persistent bullying, but these cases may be particularly recalcitrant.

B   Bullying is clearly unpleasant, and can make the child experiencing it feel unworthy and depressed. In extreme cases it can even lead to suicide, though this is thankfully rare. Victimised pupils are more likely to experience difficulties with interpersonal relationships as adults, while children who persistently bully are more likely to grow up to be physically violent, and convicted of anti-social offences.

C   Until recently, not much was known about the topic, and little help was available to teachers to deal with bullying. Perhaps as a consequence, schools would often deny the problem. 'There is no bullying at this school' has been a common refrain, almost certainly untrue. Fortunately more schools are now saying: 'There is not much bullying here, but when it occurs we have a clear policy for dealing with it.'

D   Three factors are involved in this change. First is an awareness of the severity of the problem. Second, a number of resources to help tackle bullying have become available in Britain. For example, the Scottish Council for Research in Education produced a package of materials, *Action Against Bullying*, circulated to all schools in England and Wales as well as in Scotland in summer 1992, with a second pack, *Supporting Schools Against Bullying*, produced the following year. In Ireland, *Guidelines on Countering Bullying Behaviour in Post-Primary Schools* was published in 1993. Third, there is evidence that these materials work, and that schools can achieve something. This comes from carefully conducted 'before and after' evaluations of interventions in schools, monitored by a research team. In Norway, after an intervention campaign was introduced nationally, an evaluation of forty-two schools suggested that, over a two-year period, bullying was halved. The Sheffield investigation, which involved sixteen primary schools and seven secondary schools, found that most schools succeeded in reducing bullying.

E Evidence suggests that a key step is to develop a policy on bullying, saying clearly what is meant by bullying, and giving explicit guidelines on what will be done if it occurs, what records will be kept, who will be informed, what sanctions will be employed. The policy should be developed through consultation, over a period of time – not just imposed from the head teacher's office! Pupils, parents and staff should feel they have been involved in the policy, which needs to be disseminated and implemented effectively.

Other actions can be taken to back up the policy. There are ways of dealing with the topic through the curriculum, using video, drama and literature. These are useful for raising awareness, and can best be tied in to early phases of development, while the school is starting to discuss the issue of bullying. They are also useful in renewing the policy for new pupils, or revising it in the light of experience. But curriculum work alone may only have short-term effects; it should be an addition to policy work, not a substitute.

There are also ways of working with individual pupils, or in small groups. Assertiveness training for pupils who are liable to be victims is worthwhile, and certain approaches to group bullying such as 'no blame', can be useful in changing the behaviour of bullying pupils without confronting them directly, although other sanctions may be needed for those who continue with persistent bullying.

Work in the playground is important, too. One helpful step is to train lunchtime supervisors to distinguish bullying from playful fighting, and help them break up conflicts. Another possibility is to improve the playground environment, so that pupils are less likely to be led into bullying from boredom or frustration.

F With these developments, schools can expect that at least the most serious kinds of bullying can largely be prevented. The more effort put in and the wider the whole school involvement, the more substantial the results are likely to be. The reduction in bullying – and the consequent improvement in pupil happiness – is surely a worthwhile objective.

Questions 31–34

*Choose the correct letter, **A**, **B**, **C** or **D**.*

Write the correct letter in boxes 31–34 on your answer sheet.

31   A recent survey found that in British secondary schools

   A   there was more bullying than had previously been the case.
   B   there was less bullying than in primary schools.
   C   cases of persistent bullying were very common.
   D   indirect forms of bullying were particularly difficult to deal with.

32   Children who are bullied

   A   are twice as likely to commit suicide as the average person.
   B   find it more difficult to relate to adults.
   C   are less likely to be violent in later life.
   D   may have difficulty forming relationships in later life.

33   The writer thinks that the declaration 'There is no bullying at this school'

   A   is no longer true in many schools.
   B   was not in fact made by many schools.
   C   reflected the school's lack of concern.
   D   reflected a lack of knowledge and resources.

34   What were the findings of research carried out in Norway?

   A   Bullying declined by 50% after an anti-bullying campaign.
   B   Twenty-one schools reduced bullying as a result of an anti-bullying campaign.
   C   Two years is the optimum length for an anti-bullying campaign.
   D   Bullying is a less serious problem in Norway than in the UK.

Questions 35–39

Complete the summary below.

*Choose **NO MORE THAN TWO WORDS** from the passage for each answer.*

Write your answers in boxes 35–39 on your answer sheet.

What steps should schools take to reduce bullying?

The most important step is for the school authorities to produce a **35** .... which makes the school's attitude towards bullying quite clear. It should include detailed **36** .... as to how the school and its staff will react if bullying occurs.

In addition, action can be taken through the **37** .... This is particularly useful in the early part of the process, as a way of raising awareness and encouraging discussion. On its own, however, it is insufficient to bring about a permanent solution.

Effective work can also be done with individual pupils and small groups. For example, potential **38** .... of bullying can be trained to be more self-confident. Or again, in dealing with group bullying, a 'no blame' approach, which avoids confronting the offender too directly, is often effective.

Playground supervision will be more effective if members of staff are trained to recognise the difference between bullying and mere **39** ....

Question 40

*Choose the correct letter, **A**, **B**, **C** or **D**.*

Write the correct letter in box 40 on your answer sheet.

Which of the following is the most suitable title for Reading Passage 3?

    A   Bullying: what parents can do

    B   Bullying: are the media to blame?

    C   Bullying: the link with academic failure

    D   Bullying: from crisis management to prevention

WRITING

WRITING TASK 1

You should spend about 20 minutes on this task.

> *The charts below give information about USA marriage and divorce rates between 1970 and 2000, and the marital status of adult Americans in two of the years.*
>
> *Summarise the information by selecting and reporting the main features, and make comparisons where relevant.*

Write at least 150 words.

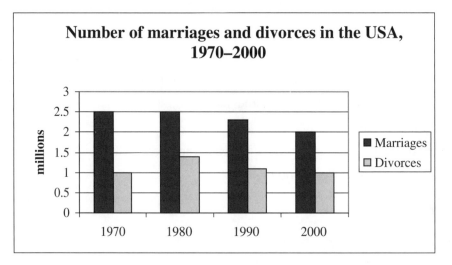

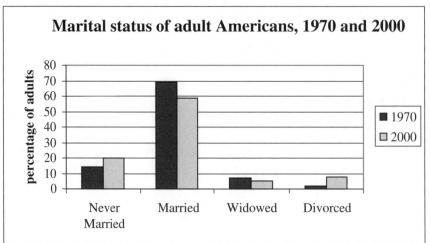

WRITING TASK 2

You should spend about 40 minutes on this task.

Write about the following topic:

> *Some people prefer to spend their lives doing the same things and avoiding change. Others, however, think that change is always a good thing.*
>
> *Discuss both these views and give your own opinion.*

Give reasons for your answer and include any relevant examples from your own knowledge or experience.

Write at least 250 words.

SPEAKING

PART 1

The examiner asks the candidate about him/herself, his/her home, work or studies and other familiar topics.

EXAMPLE

Your friends

- Do you prefer to have one particular friend or a group of friends? [Why?]
- What do you like doing most with your friend/s?
- Do you think it's important to keep in contact with friends you knew as a child? [Why/Why not?]
- What makes a friend into a good friend?

PART 2

Describe an important choice you had to make in your life.
You should say:
when you had to make this choice
what you had to choose between
whether you made a good choice
and explain how you felt when you were making this choice.

You will have to talk about the topic for one to two minutes.
You have one minute to think about what you are going to say.
You can make some notes to help you if you wish.

PART 3

Discussion topics:

Important choices

Example questions:
What are the typical choices people make at different stages of their lives?
Should important choices be made by parents rather than by young adults?
Why do some people like to discuss choices with other people?

Choices in everyday life

Example questions:
What kind of choices do people have to make in their everyday life?
Why do some people choose to do the same things every day? Are there any disadvantages in this?
Do you think that people today have more choices to make today than in the past?

General Training: Reading and Writing Test A

SECTION 1   *Questions 1–14*

Read the text below and answer Questions 1–9.

CAUSTON HEALTH CENTRE
PATIENT INFORMATION LEAFLET

A   Appointments
Please telephone 826969 (8.30am – 5.00pm: Mon – Fri). We suggest that you try to see the same doctor whenever possible because it is helpful for both you and your doctor to know each other well. We try hard to keep our appointments running to time, and ask you to be punctual to help us achieve this; if you cannot keep an appointment, please phone in and let us know as soon as possible so that it can be used for someone else. Please try to avoid evening appointments if possible. Each appointment is for one person only. Please ask for a longer appointment if you need more time.

B   Weekends and Nights
Please telephone 823307 and a recorded message will give you the number of the doctor from the Centre on duty. Please remember this is in addition to our normal working day. Urgent calls only please.
A Saturday morning emergency surgery is available between 9.30am and 10.00am. Please telephone for home visits before 10.00am at weekends.

C   Centre Nurses
Liz Stuart, Martina Scott and Helen Stranger are available daily by appointment to help you with dressings, ear syringing, children's immunisations, removal of stitches and blood tests. They will also advise on foreign travel, and can administer various injections and blood pressure checks.
For any over 75s unable to attend the clinic, Helen Stranger will make a home visit.
All three Centre Nurses are available during normal working hours to carry out health checks on patients who have been on doctors' lists for 3 years.

D   New Patients
Within 3 months of registering with the Centre, new patients on regular medication are invited to attend a health check with their doctor. Other patients can arrange to be seen by one of the Centre Nurses.

E   Services Not Covered
Some services are not covered by the Centre e.g. private certificates, insurance, driving and sports medicals, passport signatures, school medicals and prescriptions for foreign travel. There are recommended fees for these set by the National Medical Association. Please ask at reception.

F   Receptionists
Our receptionists provide your primary point of contact – they are all very experienced and have a lot of basic information at their fingertips. They will be able to answer many of your initial queries and also act as a link with the rest of the team. They may request brief details of your symptoms or illness – this enables the doctors to assess the degree of urgency.

G   Change of Address
Please remember to let us know if you decide to relocate. It is also useful for us to have a record of your telephone number.

Questions 1–4

The text on page 101 has seven sections, **A–G**.

Which section contains the following information?

*Write the correct letter, **A–G**, in boxes 1–4 on your answer sheet.*

1   what to do if you need help outside normal working hours

2   who to speak to first for general information

3   what happens when you register with the Centre

4   what to do if you need to cancel a doctor's appointment

Questions 5–9

Do the following statements agree with the information given in the text on page 101?

In boxes 5–9 on your answer sheet, write

> **TRUE**   *if the statement agrees with the information*
> **FALSE**   *if the statement contradicts the information*
> **NOT GIVEN**   *if there is no information on this*

5   You must always see the same doctor if you visit the Centre.

6   If you want a repeat prescription you must make an appointment.

7   Helen Stranger is the Head Nurse.

8   It is possible that receptionists will ask you to explain your problem.

9   You should give the Health Centre your new contact details if you move house.

Read the text below and answer Questions 10–14.

BENTLEY HOSPITAL CATERING SERVICE

TO ALL PERMANENT AND TEMPORARY MEMBERS OF STAFF

IMPORTANT INFORMATION

Meal Breaks
(minimum company guidelines)

HOURS WORKED	BREAK TO BE TAKEN
0–4 hrs	nil
4–6 hrs	15 mins
6–8 hrs	30 mins
8–12 hrs	60 mins (taken as 2 × 30 mins)
12–24 hrs	75 mins (taken as 2 × 30 mins + 1 × 15 mins)

Your section staffing board will show the times when these breaks are to be taken.

Please note
It is your responsibility to check that the total break time shown on the staffing sheets accurately reflects the breaks that you take. Any discrepancies should be raised with your Staff Co-ordinator immediately.

SPECIAL REQUIREMENTS – FOOD HANDLERS
Food handlers are those concerned with preparing and serving unwrapped food.
Food handlers should report any instance of sickness, diarrhoea and/or stomach upset experienced either while at work or during a holiday to a member of the Personnel Management team. Any infections of ear, nose, throat, mouth, chest or skin should also be reported to a member of the Personnel Management team.
Food handlers need to have an annual dental examination by the company dentist. Alternatively, a current certificate of dental fitness may be produced from their own dentist. This applies to all permanent staff who handle food.

Questions 10–14

*Complete each sentence with the correct ending, **A–J**, below.*

*Write the correct letter, **A–J**, in boxes 10–14 on your answer sheet.*

10   Temporary employees only working 3 hours should

11   Employees who work 11 hours should

12   To find out when to have their breaks, employees should

13   Employees working with food must

14   Food handlers who have been ill should

A	talk to a staff co-ordinator.
B	have two thirty-minute breaks.
C	not take any breaks for meals.
D	pay for any meals they have.
E	get a single one-hour break.
F	look at the section staffing board.
G	lose pay for their break times.
H	tell a member of the Personnel Management team.
I	have an annual dental examination.
J	consult their doctor.

SECTION 2   *Questions 15–27*

Read the text below and answer Questions 15–21.

Bramley College International Scholarships

There are seven types of scholarship offered by Bramley College to enrolled international students to assist with the costs of their courses. With the exception of applications for scholarship category E, all newly-enrolled international students are automatically considered for these scholarships. The scholarship is awarded in the student's first year as a credit to second semester course fees. In all subsequent years, the scholarship is awarded as a credit to first semester course fees. The scholarships are awarded once per year unless otherwise stated.

The scholarship categories are:

A One scholarship of A$2000 for the most outstanding students entering the Foundation Studies Program from each of the following countries: Singapore, Malaysia and Thailand. An additional six scholarships are available for students from other countries. These scholarships are offered on two dates, to students in the March and June intakes of the program. Scholarships are awarded on the basis of first semester results.

B Three scholarships providing 25% of course fees for the duration of the course to the three most outstanding State Certificate of Education (SCE) students entering a Diploma or Certificate program. Scholarships are awarded on the basis of the previous year's SCE results.

C Seventeen scholarships providing 25% of course fees for the duration of the course to outstanding Diploma or Certificate students entering each Bramley College School: three each in the Schools of Business and Engineering; two in the School of Applied Science; two in the School of Environmental Design and Construction; two in the School of Art and Design; two in the School of Social Sciences and Communications; one in the School of Biomedical and Health Science; one in the School of Education and one in the School of Nursing. Scholarships are awarded on the basis of first semester results.

D One scholarship of A$4000 per annum for the duration of the course to the most outstanding student entering the Diploma in Communication. Scholarships are awarded on the basis of first semester results.

E Nine scholarships of A$3000 per annum for the duration of the course to the most outstanding students commencing any Advanced Certificate course. Scholarships are awarded on the basis of Basic Certificate results (not SCE results). Note that applicants need to apply for this scholarship on the Bramley College International Scholarship Application Form.

F One full-fee scholarship to the most outstanding student commencing a Diploma in Art and Design (Photography) course. This scholarship is offered every second year, and is awarded on the basis of results obtained in the Certificate in Design course.

G Four half-fee scholarships to outstanding students of Bramley College's Singapore campus for the final year of the two-year Certificate in Business Studies to be completed in Melbourne, Australia. Scholarships are awarded on the basis of first year results.

Questions 15–21

*Look at the seven scholarship categories, **A–G**, on page 105.*

For which scholarship are the following statements true?

*Write the correct letter, **A–G**, in boxes 15–21 on your answer sheet.*

NB *You may use any letter more than once.*

15 It is awarded on results obtained in the SCE exam.

16 It is only available to students from the College's overseas branch.

17 It is not offered every year.

18 Students need to apply for it.

19 It is offered twice each year.

20 It pays 100% of the student's tuition fees.

21 It provides 50% of one year's fees.

Read the text below and answer Questions 22–27

Using the Internet and CD-ROM databases in the Library

Bramley College now has full electronic information resources in the College Library to help you in your studies. On CD-ROM in the library we have about fifty databases, including many statistical sources. Want to know the average rainfall in Tokyo or the biggest export earner of Vanuatu? It's easy to find out. Whether you are in the School of Business or the School of Art & Design, it's all here for you.

You can conduct your own CD-ROM search for no charge, and you can print out your results on the library printers using your library photocopying card. Alternatively, you can download your results to disk, again for no charge, but bring your own formatted floppy disk or CD-ROM. If you are not sure how to conduct a search for yourself, library staff can do it for you, but we charge $20 for this service, no matter how long or how short a time it takes.

All library workstations have broadband access to the Internet, so you can find the web-based information you need quickly and easily. If you are unfamiliar with using the Internet, help is available in several ways. You can start with the online tutorial *Netstart*; just click on the *Netstart* icon on the Main Menu. The tutorial will take you through the basic steps to using the Internet, at any time convenient to you. If you prefer, ask one of the librarians for internet advice (best at quiet times between 9.00am and 11.30am weekdays) or attend one of the introductory group sessions that are held in the first two weeks of each term. Sign your name on the list on the Library Bulletin Board to guarantee a place, as they are very popular.

A word of warning: demand for access to library workstations is very high, so you are strongly advised to book a workstation, and we have to limit your use to a maximum of one hour at any one time. Make your booking (for which you will receive a receipt) at the Information Desk or at the enquiry desks in the Media Services Area (Level 1). Also, use of the computers is limited to Bramley students only, so you may be asked to produce your Student Identification Card to make a booking, or while using the workstations.

Questions 22–27

*Choose the correct letter, **A**, **B**, **C** or **D**.*

Write the correct letter in boxes 22–27 on your answer sheet.

22 To use the library printers, students must have

   A   a floppy disk.
   B   correct change in coins.
   C   a photocopying card.
   D   their own paper.

23 To copy search results to a floppy disk, students pay

   A $20.
   B   no fee.
   C   a fee based on actual costs.
   D   a fee dependent on the time taken.

24 If library staff search for information on CD-ROM, students pay

   A $20.
   B   no fee.
   C   a fee based on actual costs.
   D   a fee dependent on the time taken.

25 Students can learn to use the Internet

   A   at all times.
   B   in the first two weeks of term only.
   C   Monday to Friday only.
   D   between 9.00am and 11.30am only.

26 To ensure efficient access to the library workstations, students should

   A   queue to use a workstation in the Media Services Area.
   B   reserve a time to use a workstation.
   C   work in groups on one workstation.
   D   conduct as many searches as possible at one time.

27 At any one time, students may use a library workstation for

   A   half an hour.
   B   one hour.
   C   two hours.
   D   an unlimited time.

SECTION 3 *Questions 28–40*

Questions 28–34

The text on pages 110 and 111 has seven paragraphs, **A–G**.

Choose the correct heading for each paragraph from the list of headings below.

*Write the correct number, **i–x**, in boxes 28–34 on your answer sheet.*

List of Headings
i   American water withdrawal
ii   Economic pricing
iii   What the future holds
iv   Successful measures taken by some
v   The role of research
vi   The thirsty sectors
vii   Ways of reducing waste
viii Interdependence of natural resources
ix   The demands of development
x   The consequences for agriculture

28   Paragraph **A**

29   Paragraph **B**

30   Paragraph **C**

31   Paragraph **D**

32   Paragraph **E**

33   Paragraph **F**

34   Paragraph **G**

THE WATER CRISIS

Greater efficiency in water use is needed to meet the growing demands of a changing world

A Per capita water usage has been on an upward trend for many years. As countries industrialise and their citizens become more prosperous, their individual water usage increases rapidly. Annual per capita water withdrawals in the USA, for example, are about 1,700 cubic metres, four times the level in China and fifty times the level in Ethiopia. In the 21st century, the world's limited supply of renewable fresh water is having to meet demands of both larger total population and increased per capita consumption. The only practicable ways to resolve this problem in the longer term are economic pricing in conjunction with conservation measures.

B Agriculture consumes about 70% of the world's fresh water, so improvements in irrigation can make the greatest impact. At present, average efficiency in the use of irrigated water in agriculture may be as low as 50%. Simple changes could improve the rate substantially, though it is unrealistic to expect very high levels of water-use efficiency in many developing countries, faced as they are with a chronic lack of capital and a largely untrained rural workforce. After agriculture, industry is the second biggest user of water and, in terms of value added per litre used, is sixty times more productive than agriculture. However, some industrial processes use vast amounts of water. For example, production of 1 kg of aluminium might require 1,500 litres of water. Paper production too is often very water-intensive. Though new processes have greatly reduced consumption, there is still plenty of room for big savings in industrial uses of water.

C In rich countries, water consumption has gradually been slowed down by price increases and the use of modern technology and recycling. In the USA, industrial production has risen fourfold since 1950, while water consumption has fallen by more than a third. Japan and Germany have similarly improved their use of water in manufacturing processes. Japanese industry, for example, now recycles more than 75% of process water. However, industrial water consumption is continuing to increase sharply in developing countries. With domestic and agricultural demands also increasing, the capacity of water supply systems is under growing strain.

D Many experts believe that the best way to counter this trend is to impose water charges based on the real cost of supplies. This would provide a powerful incentive for consumers to introduce water-saving processes and recycling. Few governments charge realistic prices for water, especially to farmers. Even in rich California, farmers get water for less than a tenth of the cost of supply. In many developing countries there is virtually no charge for irrigation water, while energy prices are heavily subsidised too (which means that farmers can afford to run water pumps day and night). Water, which was once regarded as a free gift from heaven, is becoming a commodity which must be bought and sold on the open market just like oil. In the oil industry, the price increases which hit the market in the 1970s, coupled with concerns that supplies were running low, led to new energy conservation measures all over the world. It was realised that investing in new sources was a far more costly option than improving efficiency of use. A similar emphasis on conservation will be the best and cheapest option for bridging the gap between water supply and demand.

E   One way to cut back on water consumption is simply to prevent leaks. It is estimated that in some of the biggest cities of the Third World, more than half of the water entering the system is lost through leaks in pipes, dripping taps and broken installations. Even in the UK, losses were estimated at 25% in the early 1990s because of the failure to maintain the antiquated water supply infrastructure. In addition, huge quantities of water are consumed because used water from sewage pipes, storm drains and factories is merely flushed away and discharged into rivers or the sea. The modern approach, however, is to see used water as a resource which can be put to good use – either in irrigation or, after careful treatment, as recycled domestic water. Israel, for instance, has spent heavily on used water treatment. Soon, treated, recycled water will account for most farm irrigation there. There are other examples in cities such as St Petersburg, Florida, where all municipal water is recycled back into domestic systems.

F   Another way of conserving water resources involves better management of the environment generally. Interference with the ecosystem can have a severe effect on both local rainfall patterns and water run-off. Forest clearings associated with India's Kabini dam project reduced local rainfall by 25%, a phenomenon observed in various other parts of the world where large-scale deforestation has taken place. Grass and other vegetation acts as a sponge which absorbs rainfall both in the plants and in the ground. Removal of the vegetation means that rainfall runs off the top of the land, accelerating erosion instead of being gradually fed into the soil to renew ground water.

G   Global warming is bound to affect rainfall patterns, though there is considerable disagreement about its precise effects. But it is likely that, as sea levels rise, countries in low-lying coastal areas will be hit by seawater penetration of ground water. Other countries will experience changes in rainfall which could have a major impact on agricultural yield – either for better or for worse. In broad terms, it is thought that rainfall zones will shift northwards, adding to the water deficit in Africa, the Middle East and the Mediterranean – a grim prospect indeed.

Questions 35–40

Complete the summary below.

*Choose **NO MORE THAN TWO WORDS** from the text for each answer.*

Write your answers in boxes 35–40 on your answer sheet.

Individual water usage is rising dramatically as people living in industrialised countries become increasingly **35** .... As well as increased consumption per capita, the growing demand for fresh water is due to a bigger global **36** .... than in the past. The only way to control this increase in demand is to charge high prices for water while also promoting conservation measures. Improvements in irrigation systems and industrial processes could dramatically increase the efficiency of water use. There are examples of industries in some rich countries that have reduced their consumption rates through price increases, the application of **37** .... and recycling. But in agricultural and domestic sectors, the price of water is still subsidised so it is not regarded as a commodity that people need to pay a realistic price for.

Other ways of protecting supplies are to reduce water loss resulting from **38** .... in the supply systems and to find ways of utilising used water. Longer term measures, such as improved environmental **39** .... would protect the ecosystem and ensure the replenishment of ground water for future generations. Without such measures, future supplies are uncertain, especially when global warming is expected to interfere with rainfall patterns and to worsen the **40** .... already suffered by many countries today.

WRITING

WRITING TASK 1

You should spend about 20 minutes on this task.

> *You and your family are living in rented accommodation in an English-speaking country. You are not satisfied with the condition of some of the furniture.*
>
> *Write a letter to the landlord. In your letter*
>
> * *introduce yourself*
> * *explain what is wrong with the furniture*
> * *say what action you would like the landlord to take*

Write at least 150 words.

You do **NOT** need to write any addresses.

Begin your letter as follows:

Dear .... ,

WRITING TASK 2

You should spend about 40 minutes on this task.

Write about the following topic:

> *Some people think it would be a good idea for schools to teach every young person how to be a good parent.*
>
> *Do you agree or disagree with this opinion? Describe the skills a person needs to be a good parent.*

Give reasons for your answer and include any relevant examples from your own knowledge or experience.

Write at least 250 words.

General Training: Reading and Writing Test B

SECTION 1   *Questions 1–14*

Read the text below and answer Questions 1–8.

THE EMPLOYMENT PAGES *Saturday Edition*

Australia's biggest daily selection of job ads – helping you to find the perfect position for you

Saturday Job Guide

A	Government Positions (New South Wales)
B	Higher Education (Academic staff)
C	Primary and Secondary Schools (Academic staff)
D	Hospitals and Medical (Medical staff)
E	IT and Computing
F	Accountancy and Finance (Private)
G	Hospitality and Kitchen Staff
H	Self-employment Opportunities
I	Rural Posts (incl. farm work)
J	Casual Work Available

Monday – Friday Job Highlights

TUESDAY:	Education Local Government
THURSDAY:	Hospital and Medical Government Health Vacancies (New South Wales)

Questions 1–2

Answer the questions below.

*Choose **NO MORE THAN THREE WORDS** from the text for each answer.*

Write your answers in boxes 1 and 2 on your answer sheet.

1   On which **TWO** days does the newspaper advertise jobs for teachers?

2   On which **TWO** days does the newspaper advertise jobs for nurses?

Questions 3–8

*Look at the ten categories of job advertisement, **A–J**, in the Saturday Job Guide on page 114.*

*Write the correct letter, **A–J**, in boxes 3–8 on your answer sheet.*

Which category of job advertisement should you look at if

3   you are looking for a job as a university lecturer?

4   you want to start your own business?

5   you want a permanent job in a hotel?

6   you are looking for a job in public administration?

7   you are looking for agricultural work in the country?

8   you are looking for temporary work?

Read the text below and answer Questions 9–14.

STANFIELD THEATRE

BOOKING

There are four easy ways to book seats for performances:

– in person

The Box Office is open Monday to Saturday, 10 am–8 pm.

– by post

Simply complete the booking form and return it to Stanfield Theatre Box Office, PO Box 220, Stanfield, ST55 6GF. All cheques should be made payable to **Stanfield Theatre.**

– by telephone

Ring 01316 753219 to reserve your tickets or to pay by credit card (Visa, Mastercard and Amex accepted).

– on-line

Complete the on-line booking form at www.stanfieldtheatre.com

DISCOUNTS

Saver: £2 off any seat booked any time in advance for performances from Monday to Thursday inclusive, and for all matinees. Savers are available for children up to 16 years old, over 60s and full-time students.

Supersaver: half-price seats are available for people with disabilities and one companion. It is advisable to book in advance. There is a maximum of eight wheelchair spaces available and one wheelchair space will be held until one hour before the show (subject to availability).

Standby: best available seats are on sale for £6 from one hour before the performance for people eligible for Saver and Supersaver discounts and thirty minutes before for all other customers.

Group Bookings: there is a ten per cent discount for parties of twelve or more.

Schools: school parties of ten or more can book £6 Standby tickets in advance and will get every tenth ticket free.

Please note: we are unable to exchange tickets or refund money unless a performance is cancelled due to unforeseen circumstances.

GIFT VOUCHERS

Gift vouchers for any value can be bought at the Box Office.

Questions 9–14

Do the following statements agree with the information given in the text on page 116?

In boxes 9–14 on your answer sheet, write

> **TRUE**   *if the statement agrees with the information*
> **FALSE**   *if the statement contradicts the information*
> **NOT GIVEN** *if there is no information on this*

9   It is possible to book tickets for performances using the Internet.

10 60-year-olds who want to book in advance have to prove their age to get a discount.

11 Someone accompanying a wheelchair user to a performance receives a discount.

12 Students can get Standby tickets 45 minutes before a performance begins.

13 A group of ten adults going to a performance can claim a discount.

14 Theatre-goers who are unexpectedly unable to attend a performance can get their money back.

SECTION 2   *Questions 15–27*

Questions 15–21

The text on page 119 has eight sections, **A–H**.

*Choose the correct heading for sections **B–H** from the list of headings below.*

*Write the correct number, **i–xii**, in boxes 15–21 on your answer sheet.*

List of Headings
i   Consult your teacher
ii   Take a break
iii   Make a timetable
iv   Create a working space
v   Sit comfortably
vi   Study at home
vii   Talk about your work
viii   Photocopy important material
ix   Catalogue references
x   Use the library
xi   Prioritise your work
xii   Exercise regularly

Example	*Answer*
Section **A**	**iii**

15   Section **B**

16   Section **C**

17   Section **D**

18   Section **E**

19   Section **F**

20   Section **G**

21   Section **H**

SELF-STUDY TIPS

A

However difficult you find it to arrange your time, it will pay off in the long run if you set aside a certain part of the day for studying – and stick to it. It is best to make a weekly allocation of your time, making sure that you have enough left for recreational activities or simply to be 'with' yourself: reading a novel or watching a television programme.

B

As part of your weekly schedule, it is also advisable to consider exactly what you have to do in that week, and make sure that you tackle the most significant tasks first, leaving the easier or less urgent areas of your work until later.

C

On a physical level, make sure that you have an area or space for studying. Don't do it just anywhere. If you always study in the same place, preferably a room of your own, you will find it easier to adjust mentally to the activity when you enter that area. You should have everything that you might need at hand.

D

Make sure that all the physical equipment that you use, such as a desk, chair etc. is at a good height for you. If you use a personal computer, there are plenty of guidelines available from the government on posture, angles, lighting and the like. Consult these and avoid the typical student aches and pains.

E

If you are doing a long essay or research paper which involves the use of library books or other articles, it helps to keep details of the titles and authors on small cards in a card box. It is also a good idea to log these alphabetically so that you can find them easily – rather like keeping telephone numbers. It's all too easy to read something and then forget where it came from.

F

Make use of equipment that is available to you. If you find a useful article in the library, it is best to make a copy of the relevant pages before you leave. Then, when you get back to your study, you can mark the article and make any comments that you have in the margin.

G

If you are working on a topic your teacher has set, but finding it hard to concentrate, it may be that you actually need to take your mind right off it for a period of time. 'Airing the mind' can work wonders sometimes. After a period away from the task, having not thought about it at all, you may return to it refreshed and full of ideas.

H

Similarly, it may help to discuss a topic with other people, especially if you feel that you have insufficient ideas, or too many disorganised ideas. Bring your topic up in conversations at meal times or with other students and see what they have to say. You don't want to copy their ideas but listening to what they think about something may well help you develop or refine your own thoughts.

Read the text below and answer Questions 22–27.

STUDY CENTRE COURSES

A

From Paragraph to Essay
Of particular relevance to students who wish to improve their organisational skills and who feel that their final product is never clear enough.

Thursday 10–12
Kiran Singh

B

Communicate by Mail
Owing to the popularity of last term's course, this is a repeat. Requests for information, notification of personal details and enclosures will be looked at. Please note that this is not a business course.

Friday 2–4
Celia Rice

C

Source Material
How do you gather information for a project or paper? A practical course which looks at sources of information and how to use cataloguing systems.

Monday 10–11
Kiran Singh

D

Express Yourself
An advanced course suitable for students who are about to step into organisations where they may have to voice their opinions in various forums.

Monday 12–2
Dave Parrin

E

Media Use
Open to all students, this course focuses on the many ways we can profit linguistically from the radio and television. Use of video essential. Group projects form part of course.

Tuesday 9–11
Steve Ansell

F

The Short Story
A venture into the world of popular writers. One story is selected for adaptation into a short play and group performance. Pre-arranged groups welcome.

Thursday 11–1.30
Mrs Owen

G

Caught for Speeding
Open to all students. Simple eye exercises to help you skim and scan. How to be selective on the page. Using headings, topic sentences and paragraphs for easy access.

Wednesday 11–1
Mrs Owen

H

Quote Me if You Must
The do's and don'ts of using source material. How to incorporate it into your own work in an acceptable way. How not to plagiarise other people's articles, books etc.

Tuesday 9–10.30
Dr Johnson

I

The Job for Me
Finding it, applying for it and getting it. Where can it all go wrong? Written and oral course with simulation exercises using authentic newspaper advertisements.

Friday 10–11.30
Fabbeh Al-Hussein

J

Can I Help You?
Practical course for students who wish to improve their telephone skills. Breaks the ice for newcomers. No written skills required.

Wednesday 3–5
Mike Vas

K

The Customer is Always Right
An interesting angle – how do you reply to letters from customers? What tone is best and when? How do you achieve results?

Wednesday 11–1
Celia Rice

L

Tense about Tenses
For those who worry about their individual words – a look at tenses and other aspects of the language through poetry and song. Good voice helps but not essential!

Saturday 10–12
Steve Ansell

Questions 22–27

*Look at the twelve descriptions of courses, **A–L**, on page 120.*

For which description are the following statements true?

*Write the correct letter, **A–L**, in boxes 22–27 on your answer sheet.*

22   This course would be useful for dealing with letters of complaint.

23   This course will help you use the libraries.

24   This course will improve your performance at interviews.

25   This course will help you with acknowledging your sources.

26   This course will help you improve your reading skills.

27   This course will help you improve your grammar.

SECTION 3 *Questions 28–40*

Read the text on pages 122 and 123 and answer Questions 28–40.

PTEROSAURS

Remains of the pterosaur, a cousin of the dinosaur, are found on every continent.
Richard Monastersky reports

The Pterosaur: a flying reptile that lived during the time of the dinosaur

A   Pterosaurs stand out as one of nature's great success stories. They first appeared during the Triassic period, 215 million years ago, and thrived for 150 million years before becoming extinct at the end of the Cretaceous period. Uncontested in the air, pterosaurs colonised all continents and evolved into a vast array of shapes and sizes.

B   Until recently, most scientists would not have put pterosaurs in the same class as birds in terms of flying ability. Because pterosaurs were reptiles, generations of researchers imagined that these creatures must have been cold-blooded, like modern snakes and lizards. This would have made flying awkward, as they would have lacked the endurance to power their muscles for long periods of time.

C   In the past three decades, however, a number of fossil* discoveries have prompted researchers to re-examine their views. The new picture of pterosaurs reveals that they were unlike any modern reptile. From a fossil discovered in Kazakhstan, scientists suspect that pterosaurs had a covering resembling fur. If so, this detail provides evidence of a warm-blooded body that could maintain the kind of effort needed to stay in the air. Indeed, scientists now believe that many pterosaurs were gifted airborne predators, built to feed while in flight. And, in fact, such controversy has surrounded pterosaurs since the first discovery of one in the early 1700s.

D   Cosimo Alessandro Collini, the first natural historian to study the fossil and describe it, was unable to classify it. It was not until 1791 that the great French anatomist Georges Cuvier deduced that the animal was in fact a flying reptile, whose fourth finger supported a wing. He named the fossil Pterodactylus, combining the Greek words for wing and finger. A few decades later, the name pterosaur, or winged reptile, was adopted to describe the growing list of similar fossils.

E   In 1873, a remarkable pterosaur specimen came to light that confirmed Cuvier's deduction. Unlike earlier fossils, this new find near the Bavarian town of Solnhofen contained delicate wing impressions, establishing definitely that the extinct reptile was capable of flight. Even though over a thousand pterosaur specimens are known today, such wing impressions remain rare. Normally only bones survive the fossilisation process.

F   But how pterosaurs learnt to fly remains a matter for disagreement. Most researchers conclude that pterosaurs are

---

* *fossil:* the remains or impression of a plant or animal which has been preserved in rock for a long time

descended from a small tree-dwelling reptile that spent its life jumping between branches. This creature would have spread its limbs, and used flaps of skin attached to its limbs and body to help it to land gently on the ground. Over many generations the fourth finger on each of its front 'arms' would have grown longer, making the skin surface larger and enabling the animal to glide farther. Meanwhile, the competing argument holds that pterosaurs developed from two-legged reptiles that ran along the ground, perhaps spreading their arms for balance. Through gradual growth, the front arms would then have evolved into wings. This difficult issue will only be resolved with the discovery of earlier forms of pterosaurs.

G 'It's very difficult to say how pterosaurs changed over time because the earliest fossils we have are of pterosaurs whose fourth finger has already transformed into a wing,' says Fabio dalla Vecchia, an Italian researcher. In fact, the earliest known pterosaurs came from the mountains of northern Italy, where he has spent years searching for flying reptiles. These species have shorter wings than later forms, but there is evidence that they were skilful fliers, capable of catching fish over open water. Proof of this has been found in the fossil of a *Eudimorphodon*, a 215-million-year-old pterosaur found near Bergamo, Italy. Under a microscope, several fish scales can be seen in the abdomen of the specimen – the remains of the pterosaur's last meal.

H A different but equally impressive sight is the life-size model of *Quetzalcoatlus northropi*, which stares down at visitors in the Museum of Flying in Santa Monica, California. It has a beak the size of a man and wings wider than those of many of the planes exhibited nearby. This pterosaur had wings over 11 metres wide, making it the largest flying animal ever known.

I *Quetzalcoatlus* represents the height of pterosaur evolution. 'Unlike smaller pterosaurs, it could use natural currents to stay in the air without having to move its wings continuously,' said Paul MacCready, an aeronautical engineer. 'As pterosaurs got larger, they discovered the benefits of gliding on air currents, making use of a free energy source. With their hollow bones, these pterosaurs had a very light construction, ideal for such activity.'

J As we walked beneath the *Quetzalcoatlus* model in Santa Monica, MacCready pointed out its similarity to sailplanes, the most efficient kind of aeroplanes. Both have long slender wings designed to fly with minimum power. During flight, sailplane pilots routinely search for places where heat rises from sun-baked earth, creating hot air currents called thermals. Undoubtedly, *Quetzalcoatlus* would have used thermals as well, lazily circling over the river deltas that once covered parts of Texas.

K The triumphant reign of pterosaurs ended with this giant flier. At the end of the Cretaceous period 65 million years ago, a meteorite or comet slammed into the Earth. That calamity – and other events – wiped out roughly three quarters of all species, including all pterosaurs and dinosaurs. But before their disappearance, pterosaurs enjoyed unequalled success. They flew into sunny skies before any other vertebrate. For 150 million years they sailed the winds on the strength of a fragile finger. What a glorious ride they had.

Questions 28–34

The text has eleven paragraphs, **A–K**.

Which paragraph contains the following information?

*Write the correct letter, **A–K**, in boxes 28–34 on your answer sheet.*

28   similarities between pterosaurs and mechanical flight

29   the identification of the type of creature a pterosaur actually was

30   conflicting theories about how pterosaurs came to fly

31   the cause of widespread destruction of animal life on our planet

32   the fact that pterosaurs once existed all over the world

33   the first clear proof that pterosaurs could fly

34   concrete evidence that pterosaurs hunted their food from the air

Questions 35–38

Look at the following statements (Questions 35–38) and the list of people below.

*Match each statement with the correct person, **A**, **B**, **C** or **D**.*

*Write the correct letter, **A**, **B**, **C** or **D**, in boxes 35–38 on your answer sheet.*

35   He refers to the difficulty of determining how pterosaurs evolved without further evidence.

36   He failed to interpret the evidence before him.

37   He gave an appropriate name to the first pterosaur that was discovered.

38   He mentions the ability of pterosaurs to take advantage of their environment.

List of People
A   Cosimo Alessandro Collini
B   Georges Cuvier
C   Fabio dalla Vecchia
D   Paul MacCready

Questions 39 and 40

Complete the sentences below.

*Choose **NO MORE THAN THREE WORDS AND/OR A NUMBER** from the text for each answer.*

Write your answers in boxes 39 and 40 on your answer sheet.

39   So far, evidence of a total of .... pterosaurs has been discovered.

40   The wings of *Quetzalcoatlus* measured more than .... across.

WRITING

WRITING TASK 1

You should spend about 20 minutes on this task.

> *You have just moved into a new home and are planning to hold a party.*
> *You are worried that the noise may disturb your neighbour.*
>
> *Write a letter to your neighbour. In your letter*
>
> - *introduce yourself*
> - *describe your plans for the party*
> - *invite your neighbour to come*

Write at least 150 words.

You do **NOT** need to write any addresses.

Begin your letter as follows:

Dear .... ,

WRITING TASK 2

You should spend about 40 minutes on this task.

Write about the following topic:

> *Using a computer every day can have more negative than positive effects*
> *on young children.*
>
> *Do you agree or disagree?*

Give reasons for your answer and include any relevant examples from your own knowledge or experience.

Write at least 250 words.

Tapescripts

SECTION 1

WOMAN:	Good morning, oh sorry, it's gone 12, I'll start again, good afternoon, <u>Kingswell Sports Club</u>, how can I help you? *Example*
MAN:	Oh, good afternoon. I was wondering if you could give me some information about membership and facilities.
WOMAN:	Of course. What would you like to know?
MAN:	Do you have tennis courts, for example?
WOMAN:	No, I'm afraid we don't. We're primarily a golf club.
MAN:	What about football? I heard you had a team.
WOMAN:	No, I'm sorry. Perhaps you're thinking about Fresham Sports Centre.
MAN:	Oh, right. I know it. I've played badminton there.
WOMAN:	Have you? They've got a lot of facilities we don't have and vice versa. We do have <u>a keep-fit studio</u>, which is very popular with members, *Q1* and then as well as that there's <u>swimming</u>, of course. *Q2*
MAN:	That's good. I like to swim every day.
WOMAN:	We have a range of classes too.
MAN:	Do you have judo classes? I'm keen to learn.
WOMAN:	Well, at the moment we offer kick-boxing. We're planning to add judo and stretch classes soon. We're currently running a range of <u>yoga</u> *Q3* <u>classes</u>, too.
MAN:	What about relaxing after exercise? I assume you have a restaurant or something.
WOMAN:	At the moment, we've got <u>a salad bar</u> which is very popular. We'll *Q4* also have a fully-licensed restaurant by the end of the year.
MAN:	Sounds good!

WOMAN:	What kind of membership are you interested in?
MAN:	Um I'm not really sure. What are the options?
WOMAN:	Well, there are three different membership schemes.
MAN:	I see. What's the difference?
WOMAN:	Well, the first one's called Gold, and you can use all the facilities at any time of the day or week. You can also join in as many classes as you like for free.
MAN:	That sounds good. Is it very expensive?
WOMAN:	Well, you pay a £250 joining fee and then it's £450 – oh no, I'm sorry, it's just gone up by £50, sorry about that – it's now <u>£500</u> for the annual *Q5* subscription fee.

MAN:	Right, got that. And what's the next type?
WOMAN:	Well, that's Silver – it's the same as Gold except you have to pay a small fee of £1.00 per lesson for any you do and you can only use the centre at certain times. *Q6*
MAN:	I see. So when exactly?
WOMAN:	You can only use the facilities <u>between 10 am and 4.30 pm</u>. *Q7*
MAN:	So I couldn't use the pool at 8 in the morning or evening, then?
WOMAN:	That's right.
MAN:	OK. And the price for that? Is the joining fee the same as for Gold?
WOMAN:	Actually, it's slightly less than the £250 – it's £225, but the annual fee is only £300. Does that sound more like what you want?
MAN:	Well, it's still rather more expensive than I thought. I'm a student here in England and I'm only here for six months.
WOMAN:	Ah, then the Bronze scheme would probably suit you best.
MAN:	How is that different?
WOMAN:	Well, some of the facilities have restricted use.
MAN:	And do I have to pay for classes?
WOMAN:	Yes, it's £3 for each class you join.
MAN:	I see. And what are the hours then?
WOMAN:	Between 10.30 and 3.30 weekdays only and you pay a £50 joining fee. The annual fee is <u>£180</u> – it works out at £15 a month, so that would be quite a lot cheaper. *Q8*
MAN:	Oh, that should be all right. I could come in my free periods. What do I have to do if I want to join?
WOMAN:	Well, we book you in for an <u>assessment</u> with an instructor, who will show you how to use all the equipment. If you want to organise a trial session and look around the centre, you'll need to speak to David Kynchley. *Q9*
MAN:	Hmm. Could you spell that please?
WOMAN:	Yes, David <u>K–Y–N–C–H–L–E–Y</u>. I'll give you his direct line number. It's oh–four–five–eight–nine–five–three–double one. *Q10*
MAN:	Thanks.
WOMAN:	Thank you for calling Kingswell Sports Club.

SECTION 2

MAN:	And here on Radio Rivenden we have Lynne Rawley, the Public Relations Officer of our own Rivenden City Theatre. Hello, Lynne.
LYNNE:	Hello.
MAN:	Now, the theatre is reopening soon after its three-year redevelopment programme, isn't it?

| LYNNE: | That's right, and there are a lot of improvements. The first thing people will see when they go in is that the foyer has been repainted in the original green and gold. Then the box office has been reoriented, with its own access from the side of the building instead of through the foyer, which means it can be open longer hours, and has more space, too. The shop that used to be in the foyer, which sold books and CDs, is the one part of the redevelopment which isn't yet complete. The plan is to find new premises for it near the theatre, and we've had difficulty finding somewhere suitable. We hope to reopen the shop in the next few months. | *Q11*

Q12 |

MAN: Will audiences find any difference in the auditorium?

LYNNE: Yes, we've increased the leg-room between the rows. This means that there are now fewer seats but we're sure audiences will be much *Q13* happier. And we've installed air conditioning, so it won't get so hot and stuffy. We already had a few seats which were suitable for wheelchair users, and now there are twice as many, which we hope *Q14* will meet demand. Something else that will benefit audiences is the new lifts. The two we used to have were very small and slow. *Q15* They've now gone, and we've got much more efficient ones.

MAN: Anything for the performers?

LYNNE: Yes, we've made a number of improvements backstage. The small, *Q16* dark dressing rooms we used to have have been converted into two large airy rooms, so they're much more comfortable now. And the state-of-the-art electronic sound and lighting systems have been installed.

MAN: OK, so what's the first play that audiences can see when the theatre reopens?

LYNNE: We've got a very exciting production of Peter Shaffer's *Royal Hunt of the Sun*, which is currently touring the country. That starts on October the 13th and runs till the 19th. We're experimenting a bit with *Q17* the time the curtain goes up. We used to start all our performances at 7.30, but that made it difficult for people to go home by public transport, so instead we're beginning at 7, because at 9.45, when it *Q18* finishes, there are still buses running. Tickets are already selling fast. The Friday and Saturday performances sold out almost immediately and, in fact, now there are only tickets for Monday and Thursday. *Q19*

MAN: How much are they?

LYNNE: We've introduced a simpler price structure. Ticket prices used to range from £6 to £30 but now they're all £18. They're available from the box *Q20* office, in person, by phone, fax or post, or online.

MAN: OK, Lynne, now if you'd like to give the contact details for the theatre . . .

SECTION 3

TUTOR:	Hello, can I help you?
BRIAN:	I was told to come here, because I'd like to talk to someone about taking a management course.
TUTOR:	Right. I'm one of the tutors, so I should be able to help you.
BRIAN:	Oh, good. My name's Brian Ardley. I've decided to enrol on a part-time management course. A friend of mine took one last year, and recommended it to me.
TUTOR:	Right.
BRIAN:	Is there anything I should do before the course, like reading or anything?
TUTOR:	We prefer to integrate reading with the course, so we don't give out a reading list in advance. But we like people to write a case study, describing an organisation they know.
BRIAN:	I've already done that, as my friends told me you wanted one. But would it be possible to <u>sit in on a teaching session</u>, to see what it's like? *Q21* I haven't been a student for quite a while.
TUTOR:	Fine. Just let me know which date, and I'll arrange it with the tutor.
BRIAN:	Now, could I ask you about the college facilities, please?
TUTOR:	Anything in particular?
BRIAN:	Well, the course is one day a week, all day, isn't it? So presumably it's possible to buy food?
TUTOR:	Yes, the refectory's open all day.
BRIAN:	Does it cater for special diets? I have some food allergies.
TUTOR:	Provided you warn the refectory <u>in advance</u>, it won't be a problem. *Q22*
BRIAN:	Good. What about facilities for young children? I'd like to bring my daughter here while I'm studying.
TUTOR:	How old is she?
BRIAN:	Three.
TUTOR:	Then she's eligible to join the <u>nursery</u>, which is supervised by a qualified *Q23* Nursery Nurse. The waiting list for a place is quite long though, so you ought to apply now.
BRIAN:	OK.
TUTOR:	I don't know if our careers advice service would be of any interest to you?
BRIAN:	Yes, it might help me decide how to develop my career after the course.
TUTOR:	The centre has a lot of reference materials, and staff qualified to give guidance on a one-to-one basis.
BRIAN:	I noticed a fitness centre next to the college. Is that for students?
TUTOR:	It's open to everyone, but students pay an <u>annual fee</u> that's much less *Q24* than the general public pay.
BRIAN:	And presumably the college library stocks newspapers and journals, as well as books?
TUTOR:	Yes, and there's also an audio-visual room, for viewing and listening to videos, cassettes, and so on.

BRIAN:	Is there also access to computers?
TUTOR:	Yes, your <u>tutor</u> will need to arrange with the technical support team for *Q25*
	you to get a password, so ask him or her about it when you start the course.
BRIAN:	OK.

TUTOR:	By the way, do you know about our Business Centre?
BRIAN:	No. What's that?
TUTOR:	It's a training resource – a collection of materials for people to study on
	their own, or use in their own organisations.
BRIAN:	Uhuh. You mean books and videos?
TUTOR:	Yes, and manuals for self-study. Plus a lot of computer-based materials,
	so people can work through them at their own speed, and repeat anything
	they aren't sure about. And you can hire <u>laptops</u> to use in your own *Q26/27*
	home or workplace as well as <u>printers</u> that you can take away. *Q26/27*
BRIAN:	Does it have anything that I could use to improve my study skills? I don't
	have much idea about <u>report writing</u>, and I'm sure I'll need it on the *Q28*
	course.
TUTOR:	Oh yes, there's plenty of useful material. Just ask one of the staff.
BRIAN:	Does the centre cover all the main areas of business?
TUTOR:	Yes, topics like finance, and of course <u>marketing</u> – that's a popular one. *Q29*
	Local managers seem to queue up to borrow the videos!
BRIAN:	So it isn't just for students, then?
TUTOR:	No, it's for members only, but anyone can join.
BRIAN:	How much does it cost?
TUTOR:	£100 a year for a company, and £50 for an <u>individual</u>, with no discount *Q30*
	for students, I'm afraid.
BRIAN:	That's very helpful. Well, I think that's all. I'd better go home and fill in
	the enrolment form. Thanks for all your help.
TUTOR:	You're welcome. Goodbye.
BRIAN:	Goodbye.

SECTION 4

In the last few weeks, we've been looking at various aspects of the social history of London, and this morning we're continuing with a look at life in the area called the East End. I'll start with a brief history of the district, and then focus on life in the first half of the twentieth century.

Back in the first to the fourth centuries AD, when the Romans controlled England, London grew into a town of 45,000 people, and what's now the East End – the area by the river Thames, and along the road heading north-east from London to the coast – consisted of farmland with crops and livestock which helped to <u>feed</u> that population.   *Q31*

The Romans left in 410, at the beginning of the fifth century, and from then onwards the country suffered a series of invasions by tribes from present-day Germany and Denmark, the Angles, Saxons and Jutes, many of whom settled in the East End. The technology they introduced meant that <u>metal</u> and <u>leather</u> goods were produced there for the first time. And as   *Q32* the East End was by the river, ships could transport goods between there and foreign markets.

In the eleventh century, in 1066 to be precise, the Normans conquered England, and during the next few centuries London became one of the most powerful and prosperous cities in Europe. The East End benefited from this, and because there were fewer <u>restrictions</u> there   *Q33* than in the city itself, plenty of newcomers settled there from abroad, bringing their skills as workers, merchants or money-lenders during the next few hundred years.

In the sixteenth century the first dock was dug where <u>ships</u> were constructed, eventually   *Q34* making the East End the focus of massive international trade. And in the late sixteenth century, when much of the rest of <u>England</u> was suffering economically, a lot of agricultural   *Q35* workers came to the East End to look for alternative work.

In the seventeenth century, the East End was still a series of separate, semi-rural settlements. There was a shortage of accommodation, so marshland was drained and <u>built</u> on to house   *Q36* the large numbers of people now living there.

By the nineteenth century London was the busiest port in the world, and this became the main source of employment in the East End. Those who could afford to live in more pleasant surroundings moved out, and the area became one where the vast majority of people lived in extreme <u>poverty</u>, and suffered from appalling sanitary conditions.   *Q37*

That brief outline takes us to the beginning of the twentieth century, and now we'll turn to housing.

At the beginning of the century, living conditions for the majority of working people in East London were very basic indeed. <u>Houses were crowded closely together and usually very</u>   *Q38/39/40* <u>badly built</u>, because there was no regulation. But the poor and needy were attracted by the possibility of work, and they had to be housed. It was the availability, rather than the condition, of the housing that was the major concern for tenants and landlords alike.

<u>Few houses had electricity at this time, so other sources of power were used, like coal for</u>   *Q38/39/40* <u>the fires which heated perhaps just one room</u>. Of course, the smoke from these contributed a great deal to the air pollution for which London used to be famous.

<u>A tiny, damp, unhealthy house like this might well be occupied by two full families, possibly</u> *Q38/39/40* <u>including several children, grandparents, aunts and uncles</u>.

Now, before I go on to health implications of this way of life, I'll say something about food and nutrition.

TEST 2

SECTION 1

MAN:	Good morning, Synmouth Museum. Can I help you?
WOMAN:	Oh yes. Good morning. I'm interested in the children's workshops and I'd like a little more information, please.
MAN:	Do you mean the Art and Craft workshops?
WOMAN:	Yes. A friend of a friend mentioned them – the children do painting and make models and so forth.
MAN:	Yes, of course. Um, where to begin? First of all, as you probably know, they run every <u>Saturday</u>. *Example*
WOMAN:	Fine. And what about ages?
MAN:	Well, all ages from five upwards are welcome, though we do ask that children below <u>eight</u> years of age are accompanied by an adult. *Q1*
WOMAN:	Fine. That wouldn't be a problem. What about cost?
MAN:	Well, I think you'll find them very reasonable. It's £2.50 a child, with 80 pence off for two or more children from the same family.
WOMAN:	Oh yes, very reasonable. And are they held in the main museum?
MAN:	Not exactly. They're nearby.
WOMAN:	Could you give me the full address? I don't know the area very well.
MAN:	Yes, it's Winter House.
WOMAN:	Right.
MAN:	And that's in Tamer Street.
WOMAN:	Could you spell that please?
MAN:	Yes, <u>T–A–M–E–R</u> Street. *Q2*
WOMAN:	Lovely.
MAN:	And I do need to tell you that there's a security entrance, so you need to press the <u>green button</u> for someone to let you in. Don't press the red *Q3* button please, but don't worry, it's all clearly labelled.
WOMAN:	OK. And one more question – is parking available nearby? We're driving in from out of town.
MAN:	Your best bet is to leave your car at the back of the <u>library</u> – on a *Q4* Saturday morning there are plenty of spaces there. It's right next door to the museum.
WOMAN:	And can I ask about booking places?
MAN:	Yes, and I must tell you, you really should book by calling the <u>education department</u> here. *Q5*
WOMAN:	Oh, I'm sorry, should I have rung them instead of the main museum number?
MAN:	No, that's fine this time, please don't worry. But for future reference, I'll give you the direct number. It's two hundred–seven–six–five.
WOMAN:	Great, I've got that.

133

MAN:	But I'm very happy to give you information about the next two workshops. On Saturday the 16th there's Building <u>Castles</u>.	*Q6*
WOMAN:	Oh, sounds great!	
MAN:	This involves quite a bit of glue, so just make sure the kids are in <u>old clothes.</u>	*Q7*
WOMAN:	I know, ones I don't mind getting mucky.	
MAN:	Exactly. And if possible, could you bring along <u>bottle tops</u> which the children might be able to use in the models, you know, as decoration?	*Q8*
WOMAN:	We'll certainly try to find some for you.	
MAN:	Then the following week . . .	
WOMAN:	That'll be the 23rd, won't it?	
MAN:	Yes, that's right. On that day, it's what we call <u>Undersea Worlds</u>. This is where they make scenes with fishes, underground caverns and so on.	*Q9*
WOMAN:	Is that likely to get very dirty? Lots of paint splashes?	
MAN:	Not really, so we don't recommend any special clothes for that one. But if you could search out some <u>silver paper</u> to bring along to use in the sessions, you know, it's shiny – it looks like water, that'd be great.	*Q10*
WOMAN:	Yes, of course. We'll see what we can come up with. Well, thank you ever so much for all your help. The sessions sound really good and I'll certainly book up for the next two.	
MAN:	Lovely. Thanks very much for ringing.	
WOMAN:	Bye.	
MAN:	Bye-bye.	

SECTION 2

CUSTOMER:	Hello. Um my family and I are staying here in Trebirch for a week or two and we wanted to know about the train services. We're hoping to do a few local trips.	
RAILPERSON:	OK. Well, I can give you lots of details about all the trains going from Trebirch in the South West. This leaflet will be very helpful but I can tell you some of the main things. We've got two main train stations in the town. <u>King Street</u> is for local commuter lines and regional services.	*Q11*
CUSTOMER:	What about trains to London? I'll need to go there on business for one day.	
RAILPERSON:	Then you need to go to <u>Central</u> Station – that's for all the national services. There are regular trains to London. They leave Trebirch every <u>half hour</u> on weekdays and every hour at weekends. It takes about two hours, a bit longer on Sundays. You've got a choice of first and second class and there's a buffet car – though <u>refreshments</u> are included in the cost of a first class ticket.	*Q12* *Q13* *Q14*
CUSTOMER:	Ah right. Um, and have you got any information on different ticket types?	
RAILPERSON:	Yes. There's a range of ticket prices depending on when you travel and when you buy your ticket. There's a standard open ticket which doesn't have any restrictions. This can be bought in advance or on the day. You	

can also get various discounted tickets. A popular one is called the Supersave and, er, this is OK for travel after 8.45. Then there is the Special ticket, which is valid for travel after <u>10.15</u>. The Special tickets *Q15* are also valid for travel at weekends. The cheapest tickets are called <u>Advance</u> and you have to buy them at least six days ahead. Only a certain *Q16* number are available and you have to make <u>seat reservations</u> for these. *Q17*

CUSTOMER:	Thanks. And are there lots of places to go to around here?	
RAILPERSON:	Oh yes. You can enjoy many days out. Um there's the Merthyr <u>Mining</u> <u>Museum,</u> which is only half an hour from Trebirch by train. Your children will find it just as fascinating as any theme park and they can ride in the original miners' lifts and on the coal trains. There are special excursion tickets which include entrance fees. Mainline trains also offer direct services to Bristol, where you can visit the docks or spend a great day out with the children in the <u>zoo</u>, which is set in the parkland that used to surround the old castle. Er, special family awayday fares are available for this service now during the school holidays. Er, alternatively, you can be in Birmingham in only an hour and a half, where there's lots to see and do including the new and internationally-acclaimed <u>climbing wall</u> built on the site of the old aquarium. We will also be running a special service to Newport when the new science museum opens next year, as we anticipate a lot of visitors in the opening weeks. I'd advise you to call early to book your tickets. Is that OK?	*Q18/19/20* *Q18/19/20* *Q18/19/20*
CUSTOMER:	Yes, thanks.	

SECTION 3

TUTOR:	Hello, Sandy. How have you been getting on with your dissertation?	
SANDY:	Fine, and I've been working hard on the various action points we agreed on our last tutorial.	
TUTOR:	Do you want to talk me through what you've done?	
SANDY:	Yeah, sure. Well, we agreed on three main targets for me to aim for. The first one was to find out about suitable data analysis software.	
TUTOR:	Yes.	
SANDY:	And what I decided to do was to look through <u>catalogues</u> specialising in IT.	*Q21*
TUTOR:	That's a good idea. What did you come up with?	
SANDY:	I found the names of two promising ones.	
TUTOR:	Right.	
SANDY:	But I also thought it'd be worthwhile talking to a lecturer.	
TUTOR:	Oh right. Who did you see?	
SANDY:	Jane Prince. Do you know her? She's in the <u>Computer Centre</u>.	*Q22*
TUTOR:	Yes, of course, she's the new Head.	
SANDY:	Yes. Well, she was very helpful.	

TUTOR:	Oh, that's good. Did she suggest anything in particular?	
SANDY:	Yeah. She recommended software called Vivat and said I should book up for a couple of practice sessions using Vivat.	
TUTOR:	Great. I'm sure you'll find them useful.	
SANDY:	And, of course, the second target was to draw up a survey <u>checklist</u> which I . . .	Q23
TUTOR:	Yes, you emailed me it last week.	
SANDY:	Have you had a chance to look . . .?	
TUTOR:	Of course, um I think it's good. Very much on the right lines. I'd say your first two sections are spot on. I wouldn't suggest that you change anything there, but in section three you really do need to have questions on <u>teaching experience</u>.	Q24
SANDY:	Yeah. I was thinking that section looked a bit short.	
TUTOR:	Right.	
SANDY:	And my third target was, do further reading on discipline.	
TUTOR:	Oh yes. I mentioned a couple of writers, didn't I?	
SANDY:	Yes, well I got hold of the Banerjee and I thought that was excellent. But I'm afraid I didn't manage to get hold of the essays about <u>classroom</u> management – you know, the ones by Simon Ericsson. The bookshop said it was out of print and the library doesn't have a copy.	Q25
TUTOR:	Oh right, and I'm afraid I've lent my copy to another student. What I suggest you do is try the library again – this time apply for it through the service called special loans. Have you done that before? You're entitled to six books a year.	
SANDY:	Yes. No problem. That's what I'll do.	
TUTOR:	So, lots of useful work done.	

TUTOR:	So, let's look at some new targets. We'll start by having a chat about your Chapter One. I very much enjoyed reading it. Your written style is very clear and you've included lots of interesting descriptions of education in your target area. I've just got a couple of suggestions for some additional work.	
SANDY:	Of course. Could I just ask – what do you think I should call it?	
TUTOR:	Well, I'd go for something like *Context <u>Review</u>*. What do you think?	Q26
SANDY:	Well, short and to the point.	
TUTOR:	Exactly. Now, as regards specific areas to work on, I'd be quite interested to have a few more statistics about the <u>schools</u> in the different zones.	Q27
SANDY:	Oh, that wouldn't be a problem. I can get them from the Internet.	
TUTOR:	Great, and although you did make a reference to quite a few different writers, I think you should aim to cite more works written later than <u>2000</u>.	Q28
SANDY:	OK. That's more difficult, but I can try. When do you want that done by?	
TUTOR:	Oh, it's not urgent. Um I should aim for the <u>end of term</u>. But in the meantime, I think you should also be thinking about Chapter Two.	Q29

SANDY:	Should I be drafting it already?
TUTOR:	No, but I think you should note down its main sections.
SANDY:	Yes. You know, I always find that the hardest part.
TUTOR:	I always find it helpful to put some ideas on index cards.
SANDY:	Yeah.
TUTOR:	Um . . . and then you can sort them, and even lay them out on the floor. It's a real help.
SANDY:	Well, I'll certainly try it! When would the deadline be for that?
TUTOR:	My advice would be to get it done before you embark upon the <u>research</u>. You can always change it later if you need to. *Q30*
SANDY:	OK. I'll get going on that then.

SECTION 4

Many believe that the story first began in America in 1877, when two friends were arguing over whether a horse ever had all four feet or hooves off the ground when it galloped. To settle the bet, a photographer was asked to photograph a horse galloping and the bet was settled because you could see that <u>all the hooves were off the ground in some of the photos</u>. *Q31* What was even more interesting was that if the photos were shown in quick succession the horse looked like it was running – in other words 'moving pictures'.

The person who became interested in taking the moving pictures to its next step was the famous American inventor Thomas Edison. Actually, he didn't do the work himself but rather asked a young Scotsman in his employ to design a system, which he did. Now this young fellow was clever because the first thing he did was study other systems – primitive as they were – of moving pictures and then <u>put all the existing technologies together to make</u> *Q32* <u>the first entire motion picture system</u>. He designed a camera, a projection device and the film. The system was first shown in New York in 1894 and was really very popular. Apparently people lined up around the block to see the wonderful new invention. There were, however, a couple of problems with the system. <u>The camera weighed over 200 kilograms</u> and only *Q33* one person at a time could see the film.

Well now, news of the new system in America travelled fast and <u>a number of rival European</u> *Q34* <u>systems started to appear once people had heard about it</u>. The single problem with all the systems was they couldn't really project the film onto a screen – you know, so more than one person could see it. <u>Then in 1895, three systems were all developed, more or less at the same</u> *Q35* <u>time and independently of each other. I guess the most famous of these was by the Lumière Brothers from France</u>, and they called their system the *cinematographe* which of course is where the word cinema comes from. There were also two brothers in Germany who developed a successful system and they called it a *bioskop*.

Well now, once the problem of projection had been solved, the next challenge for the inventors was to make the films longer and more interesting. A continuing problem at the time was that the <u>films had a tendency to break when they were being played – a problem</u> *Q36* <u>which was caused by the tension between the two wheels, or 'reels' as they are called, which</u>

hold the film. Now this problem was solved by two American brothers. They developed the 'Lantham Loop', which was the simple addition of a third reel between the two main reels, and this took all the tension away with the result that the film stopped snapping.   *Q37*

So now there was a real possibility of having films of more than two or three minutes, and this led to the making of *The Great Train Robbery* – the very first *movie* made. It only   *Q38* lasted 11 minutes but was an absolute sensation, and there were cases of people watching the movie and actually fainting when the character fired a gun at the camera! Almost overnight movies became a craze, and by 1905 people in America were lining up to see movies in 'store theatres', as they were called then.

I guess the next big step in terms of development of technology was to have people actually talking on the film, and the first step towards this was in 1926 when sound effects were first   *Q39* used on a film. It wasn't until the following year however that the first 'talkie', as they were called then, was made. This film featured actors speaking only during parts of the film and was called *The Jazz Singer*, and it wasn't until 1928 that the first all-talking film was produced, and this was called *The Lights of New York*. Unfortunately, the sound on this early film was not very good and I believe they put subtitles on the film – that is, they printed the dialogue along the bottom of the film to compensate for this poor sound   *Q40* quality. Now, with the addition of sound, moving pictures became far more difficult to make . . .

TEST 3

SECTION 1

PIETER:	Good morning. I'd like to open a bank account, please.	
WOMAN:	Certainly. If you'd like to take a seat, I'll just get some details from you. It won't take long.	
PIETER:	Thanks.	
WOMAN:	Is it a current account or a deposit account you wanted?	
PIETER:	A current account.	*Example*
WOMAN:	Right. I've got the application form here then. We have different types – I see you've got our leaflet there.	
PIETER:	I've decided on the one called 'Select.'	*Q1*
WOMAN:	Right, that's fine, so, first of all, can I have your full name please?	
PIETER:	Yes, it's Pieter Henes. That's P–I–E–T–E–R.	
WOMAN:	Is it H–E–double N–E–S?	
PIETER:	Uh, only one N actually. It's a less common spelling of the name.	
WOMAN:	Oh, right. OK. And what's your date of birth please?	
PIETER:	The twenty-seventh of the first, nineteen seventy-three.	*Q2*
WOMAN:	Right. And will this be a joint account?	
PIETER:	No, just myself.	
WOMAN:	OK, fine. And where are you living, Mr Henes?	
PIETER:	15, Riverside.	*Q3*

WOMAN:	Is that all one word?
PIETER:	Yes.
WOMAN:	Exeter?
PIETER:	Yes.
WOMAN:	How long have you been at your present address? Er, is it more than two years?
PIETER:	Ah, just <u>two weeks</u> actually. I only arrived in the country a month ago. *Q4* I'm from Holland.
WOMAN:	Oh, that's fine. But we normally ask for a previous address in that case.
PIETER:	Oh yes, well, it's Rielsdorf 2. That's R–I–E–L–S–D–O–R–F 2, Utrecht.
WOMAN:	Holland. OK. Thank you. Do you have a daytime telephone number?
PIETER:	Yes, I think the number at my office is <u>six–oh–six–two–nine–five.</u> Um, *Q5* <u>just a minute, I'd better check. Oh, no sorry, six–one–six.</u> I'm not used to it yet. Would you like my home number too?
WOMAN:	Yes please.
PIETER:	It's seven–nine–six–four–three–one.
WOMAN:	Are they both local numbers?
PIETER:	Yes.

WOMAN:	Right. And your occupation?
PIETER:	Well, I'm in Britain as a project manager, but that's not my main job. I'm an <u>engineer</u> by profession. *Q6*
WOMAN:	I see. I think I'll put that then. It's shorter! Now we usually ask for a piece of information which we can use to check your identity, for security reasons. You know, if you phone us.
PIETER:	Like, erm, my wife's first name?
WOMAN:	<u>Mother</u>'s might be better. It's less likely to be known. *Q7*
PIETER:	OK. Hers is Siti.
WOMAN:	Siti?
PIETER:	Yes, S–I–T–I. It's Indonesian.
WOMAN:	Fine. And how much would you like to open your account with? We usually ask for a minimum sum of £50. That's about €75.
PIETER:	Well, I'm going to transfer <u>€2,000</u> from my Dutch account, just till I get *Q8* paid. In fact, I wanted to ask you about that. What's the best way to do it?
WOMAN:	It depends which bank you're with.
PIETER:	It's the Fransen Bank in Utrecht.
WOMAN:	OK, fine. I'll check that in a minute. If we have links with them we can do a direct transfer. But it's not a big problem either way. Um, let's see. How often would you like to receive statements?
PIETER:	I haven't really thought. Um, what's the usual thing?
WOMAN:	It's up to you. Some people like them weekly.
PIETER:	Oh, no, that's too often. Can I have them sent, um, once a <u>month</u>? *Q9*
WOMAN:	Yes, that's fine. Is there anything else?

PIETER:	I was thinking of registering for your <u>internet</u> service at some stage.	*Q10*
WOMAN:	Oh, yes. Would you like me to send you information about that?	
PIETER:	Please, yes.	
WOMAN:	And would you like to receive information about the bank's other services – insurance, loans, anything like that?	
PIETER:	Hmm, I don't think so, thanks.	
WOMAN:	That's OK then. And one last thing, if you agree . . .	

SECTION 2

Welcome, everybody, to the lovely house and gardens of Rosewood, once the home of the famous writer, Sebastian George. He bought the house in 1902 although he had first seen it two years earlier. At that time the owners let it out to a tenant because <u>George was too</u>   *Q11*
<u>slow making up his mind to buy it</u>. When it came back on the market, there was no hesitation and he bought it immediately, for £9,300, even though the house had no bathroom, no running water upstairs, and no electricity.

When he came here, he'd been married for ten years. During that time, he'd become one of the most famous writers in the English-speaking world. His professional success was enormous, but <u>his personal life wasn't as successful. He was no longer on speaking terms</u>   *Q12*
<u>with his brother and had been devastated by the death at the age of seven of his elder</u>
<u>daughter, Josephine</u>.

Moving to Rosewood allowed the family to start a new life. <u>George regarded Rosewood</u>   *Q13*
<u>as a pure example of a traditional country house of this part of England</u> and did some of his most successful writing here. The house and its grounds became the family haven and their escape to privacy and quiet. The walls, and the mullioned windows were built of the local sandstone, the tiles on the roofs and the bricks of the chimney stack were baked from local clay, and the wooden structures inside came from oak trees which grow around here.

Now, please look at the map I've given you of the house and gardens. We're here at the Information Centre. Follow the path marked with the arrow and the first area you come to is the orchard on your left.

As you go further down the path, there's the kitchen garden on the right and <u>as you go</u>   *Q14*
<u>round the first sharp corner you will find, to your left, an area where different types of pear</u>
<u>tree have been planted as well as some lovely flowers, and this is known as Pear Alley</u> –
designed by George himself.

Next to this is the greenhouse where some exotic plants and fruits are grown. <u>Follow the</u>   *Q15*
<u>path round the second corner and on your right you will see the entrance to the Mulberry</u>

Garden with its 500-year-old tree. Past the Mulberry Garden, follow the path until you reach the front of the house. I suggest you spend a good hour wandering around this lovely building. A guide takes visitor groups round every two hours.

If you would like to purchase any of George's books or other souvenirs, then leave the   *Q16*
house by the side entrance, where you will find our shop, which is situated between the
house and the garage which contains the magnificent old Rolls-Royce car which used to
belong to George. I expect by this time you may also be in need of a rest and some
refreshment. Most visitors are, so why don't you visit the tea room on the far side of the   *Q17*
garage?

If you have time, there is a lovely walk down towards the River Dudwell. For me, this is the
best part of the estate. This isn't on the map but it is all clearly signposted. You cross the
field which spreads along the banks of the river. In spring, this area is well worth a visit.   *Q18*
Spend a minute or two watching the water pass by underneath as you cross the footbridge,   *Q19*
and then continue along the River Walk through the woodland. On a hot summer's day the
trees along this path provide welcome shade. Eventually you come to the water mill which
used to provide the electricity for the house – only about four hours every evening – in
George's time. And, finally, for those of you who would like to see stunning views of the
surrounding countryside and who are a little bit more energetic, when you return from
the mill take the first turning on your left and climb up to the viewpoint. You won't   *Q20*
regret it.

Enjoy your visit!

SECTION 3

JACK:	Lucy, we really need to get working on this marketing assignment. We've only got five weeks left to the end of term to design it, carry it out, and then write up the results.
LUCY:	Sure. Well, let's get started right now. Let's go over the instructions. What exactly do we have to do?
JACK:	Well, it says here we have to look at one area of the entertainment *Q21* industry. There's a list of the different types.
LUCY:	What are they?
JACK:	Music, cinema, theatre, sport, and eating out.
LUCY:	Is that all?
JACK:	Looks like it.
LUCY:	So we choose one branch of the industry and then we look at how two different groups of people use it? Is that right?
JACK:	Yes.
LUCY:	And do we have to use any particular method to get our data? Can we mail out a questionnaire, or do face-to-face interviews, or maybe even observations?

JACK:	Well actually, it looks like we don't have a choice. We have to do <u>telephone interviews</u>.	*Q22*
LUCY:	OK, so at least we don't have to waste time deciding between the different methods.	
JACK:	Yeah, that's right. Oh, and the other requirement is the number of interviewees.	
LUCY:	Not too many, I hope. Ten? Twenty?	
JACK:	Well, we have to do two groups, remember, and it looks like we have to interview fifteen for each group.	
LUCY:	That's <u>thirty</u> altogether then. It's going to take ages.	*Q23*
JACK:	Yes, but remember we're working on this together, so we'll only have to do fifteen each.	
LUCY:	OK, so those are all the requirements?	
JACK:	Yes, looks like it.	
LUCY:	So, first, which area are we going to choose? My preference would be cinema, since that's where I spend most of my money.	
JACK:	Hmm, I don't think that's such a good idea. I don't think there are huge differences in the market there. I mean you get young and old, male and female, rich and poor all going to the same movies.	
LUCY:	Yeah, maybe you're right. Let's make it music then.	
JACK:	Right. So, what two groups will we compare and contrast?	
LUCY:	<u>Male and female</u>?	*Q24*
JACK:	No. Most of my female friends like the same music as me. Different age groups would be much more likely to show up differences, I think.	

LUCY:	Yeah, I suppose you're right again. I'll take some notes, shall I? So. . . Age Groups. Well. What do you think? Maybe twenty-five or under for one group, and forty-five or over for the other group? That should show up differences.	
JACK:	Right.	
LUCY:	OK. Next. How about the kind of music they like – let's give them some choices and then we can just tick boxes.	
JACK:	OK. Let's have pop, <u>jazz</u>, folk, easy listening . . . What else?	*Q25*
LUCY:	Well, we should include <u>classical</u>. Some people like it, you know.	*Q26*
JACK:	OK. OK. And then we should have how they listen to music.	
LUCY:	The medium. Right. Let's include radio, CD – and then I guess there's TV.	
JACK:	What about <u>concerts</u>? You know, in pubs and halls.	*Q27*
LUCY:	Oh yeah, we should include live music of course.	
JACK:	OK, we're on a roll now! Next point could be about where they actually get their music.	

LUCY:	You mean like, do they buy it in music shops, or <u>department stores</u>?	*Q28*
JACK:	Yes, or download it from the Internet.	
LUCY:	Right. That could be for recorded music. Then we need another section for live music. Where do they go for that?	
JACK:	OK. Let's say disco, pub, <u>club</u>, concert hall . . .	*Q29*
LUCY:	Or <u>opera house</u>! And I guess we should include karaoke bars.	*Q30*
JACK:	Not many of them in this city!	
LUCY:	OK. We'll leave that out then. So, what's left to do?	
JACK:	That's it. Well, now we can make a time-scale for doing it.	

SECTION 4

Good morning everyone. Last week we were looking at the hunter-gatherers in Ireland, across the Irish Sea from England. Today, we're going to move on to the period between four and six thousand years ago, known as the Neolithic period, which is when a total farming economy was introduced in Ireland.

Now, <u>there are several hypotheses about the origins of the first Neolithic settlers in Ireland,</u>   *Q31*
<u>but most of these contain problems</u>. For instance, there are considerable archaeological difficulties about the theory that they came from England. The evidence doesn't really add up. But there are even greater practical problems about the theory that they came directly from continental Europe. For one thing, it's not clear just how sufficient numbers of men and women could have been transported to Ireland to establish a viable population. As you know, the hunter-gatherer economy which existed beforehand was based on small scattered groups. The farming economy would almost certainly have required much larger communities to do all the work needed to plant and tend sufficient crops to sustain them through the year.

The early farmers kept various animals, including cattle and sheep. There's also evidence of pigs, but it is possible that these could have been descended from the native wild species. Now, we know from modern farming that if the level of breeding stock falls below about three hundred females, the future of the species locally is at risk. So we must assume that <u>from the beginnings of Neolithic farming the number of breeding sheep would have</u>   *Q32*
<u>considerably exceeded three hundred, and the national cattle herd must have been of a</u>
<u>similar size</u>. The question is how these were brought to the area and where they came from.

It's usually suggested that the <u>Neolithic settlers used skin-covered boats to transport</u>   *Q33*
<u>livestock. But this method would have severely restricted the range of the colonising fleets.</u>
The sheer volume of animal transport necessary means it's unlikely that this livestock could have been brought from anywhere further than England.

What about crops? Well, two main cereal crops were introduced to Ireland during this time: wheat and barley, both in several varieties. <u>The main evidence for their presence consists of</u>   *Q34*
<u>impressions on pottery, where a cereal grain accidentally became embedded in the surface</u>
<u>of a pot</u> before it was fired. The grain itself was destroyed by the firing, but it
left an impression on the pot which could be studied and identified by
botanists.

Let's turn our attention now to the farming technology available at that time. Before the cereal crops could be planted, it would have been necessary to clear the forest and to break the ground by ploughing. The stone blade of a plough has been discovered during excavation in County Mayo in western Ireland. The body of the plough would have been of wood and could have been drawn by <u>people</u>, but it's also likely that cattle   *Q35*
were used.

Now, the cultivation of crops and the husbandry of livestock brought about changes in people's lifestyle such as the type of shelters they made. For one thing, instead of moving from place to place they needed permanent dwellings. The stone axes used to chop down trees to make these dwellings were far superior to any that the Stone Age hunter-gatherers used.

To make the axes, sources of suitable stone had to be found and systematically exploited. These so-called 'axe factories' were really quarries rather than factories, as the manufacture of the axes wasn't regularly performed on the quarry site. However, after the axe had been chipped into shape, they needed <u>water</u> and <u>sand</u> for grinding and polishing, so a high   *Q36*
mountainside wouldn't have been an appropriate place for this. So this final stage of the manufacture must have been carried out close to water and sure enough, there's ample evidence of this at coastal sites.

Now it's clear that these Neolithic axes were transported all over Ireland, as well as to <u>Scotland</u> and the south of England. It's not really surprising that axes from 'axe factories'   *Q37*
in England have also been found in Ireland. At the very least, this indicates that there was a link between the two islands during that period.

One of the most useful innovations of the colonisers was pottery making, which was quite unknown to Irish hunter-gatherers. The pottery was probably made by shaping clay into a ball with the hand, and then hollowing it until the walls were the right thickness. After firing, the <u>outside</u> was often polished. This would have helped the pots to retain water, as   *Q38*
they weren't glazed. Now we know that the clay used usually came from <u>local</u> sources,   *Q39*
which suggests that manufacture was on a fairly small scale, even though thousands of fragments are usually found at Neolithic sites.

In the course of time decoration began to appear. At first this looked like a series of stitches and was just around the <u>tops</u> of the pots. This could have been an imitation of earlier vessels *Q40*
which were made of leather sewn onto wood. Then eventually pots with decoration all
over . . .

TEST 4

SECTION 1

CLERK:	Conference Centre Reservations. Good morning.	
WOMAN:	Hi. I'm interested in the computing conference next month.	
CLERK:	Future Directions in Computing?	*Example*
WOMAN:	Yes, that's right. Could I ask you a few questions about it?	
CLERK:	Of course.	
WOMAN:	OK. I know the conference is for three days but actually I want to attend on the Friday and Saturday only. Will that work out to be any cheaper?	
CLERK:	Let me have a look. Well, you could register for the two days separately, but that wouldn't actually save you very much as it still costs £35 for each day. In fact, if you could register for the three days, you also get an invitation to a free dinner on the Saturday night, so that's probably the better option.	
WOMAN:	Right, I'll do that. How much will the fees be in that case?	
CLERK:	It's £75.	*Q1*
WOMAN:	All right. I'd like to register for the full three days. Now, can I pay that by credit card?	
CLERK:	I'm afraid not. You'll have to send a cheque to us, or you can pay at the conference office.	*Q2*
WOMAN:	Fine. So it's probably easiest if I pay by cheque. Now then, what else do I need to arrange? Right. How about accommodation? I guess that's not included in the price?	
CLERK:	No, I'm sorry, it's not, but we do have a few rooms available for delegates at the conference centre if you'd like. Those are very cheap but if you're interested you'll need to book soon, because there's always a heavy demand for them. They are only £15 per night, but they are very basic and you'd have to get your own breakfast, because they don't provide you with that. But it's very convenient, because it's in the same building as the conference rooms.	*Q3*
WOMAN:	Uhuh.	
CLERK:	Or there's a very reasonable guest house which is £25 per night. And I think that includes your breakfast.	*Q4*
WOMAN:	Is it close to the conference centre?	
CLERK:	It would be about a ten-minute walk away from here.	*Q5*
WOMAN:	I see. That sounds quite reasonable.	

CLERK:	The details are all in our conference pack, which I'll send you.	*Q6*
WOMAN:	Great, thanks. That'll be very useful. Oh, and can you also send me an application form?	
CLERK:	Of course. I'll get that in the post to you straight away. Is there anything else?	

WOMAN:	Yes, actually. Can you tell me where exactly the conference centre is?	
CLERK:	Well, it's on <u>South</u> Park Road and it's right at the end of the road	*Q7*
	next to the <u>library</u>. It's a ten-minute taxi ride from the station and will	*Q8*
	cost you <u>£5</u>. Otherwise, you can take the bus which runs every half an	*Q9*
	hour from the station – that's the <u>21A</u> – and it brings you straight	*Q10*
	to the conference centre.	
WOMAN:	Right, got that.	

SECTION 2

Good morning and welcome, everybody. I'm Jenny Stewart and I'm the Staff Manager here at the exhibition centre. We're expecting this year's International Travel Exhibition to attract over 10,000 visitors a day, ladies and gentlemen, and you are among the two hundred extra staff recruited to help look after them. Now, to help things run smoothly, we have divided you into four teams – the blue team, the green team, the red team, and the yellow team. So first I'll explain how the teams are divided up, and then we'll be giving you colour-coded T-shirts so we can identify you more easily. First of all, those who will be looking after the phones and handling all calls regarding the exhibition, you will be on the red team. Now, <u>we've also put the entrance staff on the red team and you'll be stamping the entrance tickets</u> *Q11* and giving out publicity leaflets, OK?

Those of you involved in distributing entrance tickets will be on the yellow team and we've also put those of you who'll be staffing the information booths around the conference centre on the yellow team, so you'll be getting a yellow T-shirt. Now, most of the hospitality staff have been put in the blue team, so <u>the chefs among you and the kitchen hands will</u> *Q12* <u>all need a blue T-shirt</u>, but, because of the sheer numbers, all waiting staff will be on the yellow team, and this includes the bar staff among you. <u>Those who will be monitoring and</u> *Q13* <u>directing the traffic in the car parks are on the green team</u>, so you'll need to get a green T-shirt. This year we've also employed a considerable number of attendants to direct the human traffic around the conference centre. Now, you'll be working in the exhibition hall at all times, giving directions and generally helping people whenever you can, and you will be in the red team, so please collect a red T-shirt.

Right, now that everyone knows what team they're in, we'll get on with the orientation and training programme and first I'll run through the rest of today's programme, which you should have in front of you, so that you can get a general idea of what else is in store today. This introduction finishes at 9.30 and then you'll be hearing from Anne Smith. Anne works in the accounts department on level two and she looks after all temporary staff, and so she is the person to see if you have any problems regarding pay. Anne will be explaining when and how you get this. She will also be handing out your <u>tax</u> forms. And I will just *Q14* stress that all tax forms must be completed and returned to Anne before your pay can be processed. Following Anne's talk you'll hear from Peter Chen, our Conference Manager, and he will be going over a plan of the conference centre with you, which will help you to

orient yourselves. He will also go through the <u>security</u> arrangements with you and show *Q15*
you the fire exits. Then at 10.30, there will be a coffee break in the staff canteen, which is
located down on the <u>ground floor</u>. Now, after the break we'll be moving to a different *Q16*
location for a video presentation, so instead of coming back here, we'd like you all to go
to <u>Lecture Room three–one–one</u>. You'll find it on this same level, just down the hall, and *Q17*
there you will be shown a video about important safety issues in the workplace, called
Safety at Work. We'll finish off the morning with lunch, which should give everyone a *Q18*
chance to meet and get to know each other, and we'll be serving you a buffet lunch in
the <u>Main Hall</u>, which is on the first floor, from 12.00 o'clock. After lunch you'll be *Q19*
divided up into your teams to meet your <u>team leaders</u> and we're hoping to be all *Q20*
finished by 3.00 so I won't delay you any longer, and I'll hand over to . . .

SECTION 3

LIBRARIAN:	Good afternoon. Can I help you?
STUDENT:	Good afternoon. Yes, I've just transferred to the School of Education, and I'd like information about joining the library.
LIBRARIAN:	Well, the School of Education has libraries on two sites, as I'm sure you know. This one here is the Fordham Site, and the other is on Castle Road.
STUDENT:	And is there any difference between the two libraries?
LIBRARIAN:	Not in terms of their facilities. Access to online databases and the Internet is available at both sites and each site has a range of <u>reference</u> materials on education.

Q21

STUDENT:	Oh yes. I see.
LIBRARIAN:	But the Castle Road site has books on the sociology of education and a collection of <u>textbooks</u> and teaching resources covering most of the subjects taught in <u>secondary</u> schools.

Q22
Q23

STUDENT:	Ah, right, but I'm training to be a primary teacher so I need to look at materials for the five to eleven age group.
LIBRARIAN:	Then you've come to the right place. At Fordham we hold material relating to <u>primary</u> education, as well as special needs, but of course you'll need to familiarise yourself with both sites to make the most of our resources.

Q24

STUDENT:	You haven't mentioned periodicals. Are they held at both sites?
LIBRARIAN:	Current issues, yes but if you want to look at <u>back</u> issues you'll need to use the CD-ROM databases which are held here at Fordham.

Q25

STUDENT:	I see. Now, about borrowing books. I'm living out of town, so I'm hoping I can borrow quite a few items, and cut down on the number of trips I have to make.
LIBRARIAN:	Right, well, members can borrow two books at a time from each site.

STUDENT:	Only two books?
LIBRARIAN:	Only two from each site, but that's four altogether.
STUDENT:	Oh I see, and how long can I hang on to them for?
LIBRARIAN:	The borrowing period is one month, but of course books can be renewed. You can renew any item a maximum of three times.
STUDENT:	Do I have to come to the library to do that?
LIBRARIAN:	No, you can do it by telephone or email, but you can't renew <u>overdue</u> books this way, only before or on the due date stamped *Q26* in the book. We'll need your full name, your borrower number and the name of the site library you borrowed the items from.
STUDENT:	So theoretically I can borrow books for up to three months – is that what you're saying?
LIBRARIAN:	Yes, provided they're not recalled.
STUDENT:	So, what happens then?
LIBRARIAN:	Well, sometimes an item is requested by another borrower, in which case we'd send you a letter, and you'd have to return the book within <u>seven working days</u>. Don't forget we're closed on *Q27* Sundays.
STUDENT:	OK.

STUDENT:	I expect it'll take me a while to find what I need. There's such a lot here.
LIBRARIAN:	Yes there is, but if you need help getting started, this term we're running three study skills workshops.
STUDENT:	Oh? What are they on?
LIBRARIAN:	Er, let me see. The first one's on resources – yes, here it is. <u>How to use the library's resources. That includes everything, not</u> *Q28/29/30* <u>just the print and technical resources.</u>
STUDENT:	That sounds useful. Is there anything on using the Internet?
LIBRARIAN:	Er, let's see. The one on the Internet for beginners was last term. <u>This</u> *Q28/29/30* <u>term it's finding research materials online.</u>
STUDENT:	That sounds interesting too, hm, what's the last one?
LIBRARIAN:	It's <u>a workshop on dissertations.</u> *Q28/29/30*
STUDENT:	<u>What do you mean – how to write one?</u>
LIBRARIAN:	<u>Er, no</u> it's more to do with academic writing conventions, you know – writing a bibliography and how to refer to sources in your text. That sort of thing. Anyway, here's a leaflet with information about all three.
STUDENT:	Thanks a lot. That'll be very useful.
LIBRARIAN:	You're welcome.

SECTION 4

Well, most people think that lions only come from Africa. And you would be forgiven for thinking this, because in fact most lions do come from Africa. But this hasn't always been the case. If we go back ten thousand years we would find that there were lions roaming vast sections of the globe. But now, unfortunately, only very small sections of the lions' former habitat remain.

My particular interest is Asiatic lions, which are a sub-species of African lions. <u>It's almost</u>   *Q31*
<u>a hundred thousand years since the Asiatic lions split off and developed as a sub-species.</u>
At one time the Asiatic lion was living as far west as Greece and they were found from there, in a band that spread east through various countries of the Middle East, all the way to India. In museums, you can now see <u>Greek coins that have clear images of the Asiatic</u>   *Q32*
<u>lion on them.</u> Most of them are dated at around 500 B.C. However, <u>Europe saw its last</u>   *Q33*
<u>Asiatic lion roaming free two thousand years ago.</u> Over the next nineteen hundred years the numbers of Asiatic lions in the other areas declined steadily, but it was only in the nineteenth century that they disappeared from everywhere but India.

So, how can you tell an Asiatic lion from an African lion, with which you're probably more familiar? Well, in general, Asiatic lions are not as big as African lions. The colour is more or less the same, but the appearance of the mane is different – that's the hair around the lion's face and neck. The Asiatic lion's mane is noticeably shorter than the African lion's. <u>Asiatic lions also have a long fold of skin on their undersides, whereas not many</u>   *Q34*
<u>African lions have this.</u>

Well, I'd like to talk to you now about the Gir Sanctuary in India. That's where I've just come back from. The sanctuary was established specifically to protect the Asiatic lion. It's <u>1,450</u> square kilometres in area and most of it is forest. There are now around   *Q35*
three hundred Asiatic lions in India and almost all of them are in this sanctuary.

But despite living in a sanctuary, which makes them safe from hunters, they still face a number of problems that threaten their survival. One of these is the ever-present danger of <u>disease</u>. This is what killed more than a third of Africa's Serengeti lions in 1994, and   *Q36*
people are fearful that something similar could happen in the Gir Sanctuary and kill off many of the Asiatic lions there.

India's lions are particularly vulnerable because they have a limited gene pool. The reason for this is interesting – it's because all of them are descended from a few dozen lions that were saved by a <u>prince</u> who took a particular interest in them. He was very wealthy, and   *Q37*
he managed to protect them – otherwise they'd probably have died out completely.

When you see the Asiatic lion in India, what you sense is enormous vitality. They're very impressive beasts and you would never guess that they had this vulnerability when you look at them.

The Asiatic lions don't have the Gir Sanctuary to themselves, I should add. They actually share it with about two thousand farmers. A significant proportion of the lions' <u>diet</u> is   *Q38* made up of the livestock of these farmers – goats, chickens and so on – as much as a third, in fact. And they've even been known to <u>attack humans</u>, especially in times of drought.   *Q39*

One final piece of interesting information – in ancient India one of the greatest tests of <u>leadership</u> for a man was to fight a lion. Now it seems, in modern India it will be a great   *Q40* test to see if the lion can be saved. I'm sure this is something that all of you will share concern for too.

Answer key

LISTENING

Section 1, Questions 1–10

1 (a) keep-fit (studio)
2 swimming
3 yoga (classes)
4 (a) salad bar
5 500
6 1
7 10 (am), 4.30 (pm)
8 180
9 assessment
10 Kynchley

Section 2, Questions 11–20

11 B
12 G
13 C
14 A
15 E
16 D
17 (October (the)) 19th
18 7
19 Monday, Thursday
20 18

Section 3, Questions 21–30

21 A
22 in advance
23 nursery
24 annual fee
25 tutor
26&27 IN EITHER ORDER
 laptops
 printers
28 report writing
29 marketing
30 Individual

Section 4, Questions 31–40

31 feed
32 **IN EITHER ORDER**
 metal
 leather
33 restrictions
34 ships
35 England
36 built
37 poverty
38–40 IN ANY ORDER
 C
 E
 F

If you score . . .

0–12	13–26	27–40
you are unlikely to get an acceptable score under examination conditions and we recommend that you spend a lot of time improving your English before you take IELTS.	you may get an acceptable score under examination conditions but we recommend that you think about having more practice or lessons before you take IELTS.	you are likely to get an acceptable score under examination conditions but remember that different institutions will find different scores acceptable.

ACADEMIC READING

Reading Passage 1, Questions 1–13

1	B
2	C
3	B
4	F
5	D
6	A
7	E
8	A
9	B
10	A
11	C
12	(a) competition model
13	(by) 2 per cent/%

Reading Passage 2, Questions 14–26

14	I
15	F
16	E
17	D
18	TRUE
19	FALSE
20	NOT GIVEN
21	TRUE
22	NOT GIVEN
23	G
24	B
25	C
26	A

Reading Passage 3, Questions 27–40

27	i
28	vi
29	iii
30	vii
31	iv
32	ii
33	farming
34&35	***IN EITHER ORDER***
	sea mammals
	fish
36	Thule
37	islands
38	nomadic
39	nature
40	Imported

If you score . . .

0–12	13–30	31–40
you are unlikely to get an acceptable score under examination conditions and we recommend that you spend a lot of time improving your English before you take IELTS.	you may get an acceptable score under examination conditions but we recommend that you think about having more practice or lessons before you take IELTS.	you are likely to get an acceptable score under examination conditions but remember that different institutions will find different scores acceptable.

TEST 2

LISTENING

Section 1, Questions 1–10

1   8
2   (in/on) Tamer
3   green button
4   library
5   education department
6   castles
7   old clothes
8   bottle tops
9   Undersea Worlds
10 silver paper

Section 2, Questions 11–20

11   King Street
12   central
13   half hour/30 minutes
14   refreshments
15   10.15
16   Advance
17   (seat) reservations
18–20   *IN ANY ORDER*
      C
      D
      G

Section 3, Questions 21–30

21   catalog(ue)s
22   computer centre/center
23   checklist
24   teaching experience
25   classroom
26   review
27   schools
28   ((the) year) 2000
29   end of term
30   research

Section 4, Questions 31–40

31   A
32   B
33   C
34   A
35   A
36   C
37   A
38   Great Train Robbery
39   Sound effects
40   poor sound quality

If you score . . .

0–13	14–28	29–40
you are unlikely to get an acceptable score under examination conditions and we recommend that you spend a lot of time improving your English before you take IELTS.	you may get an acceptable score under examination conditions but we recommend that you think about having more practice or lessons before you take IELTS.	you are likely to get an acceptable score under examination conditions but remember that different institutions will find different scores acceptable.

ACADEMIC READING

Reading Passage 1, Questions 1–13

1	ii
2	vii
3	iv
4	i
5	iii
6	FALSE
7	TRUE
8	NOT GIVEN
9	FALSE
10	TRUE
11	F
12	D
13	C

Reading Passage 2, Questions 14–26

14	B
15	I
16	F
17	M
18	J
19	N
20	K
21	G
22	A
23	G
24	E
25	H
26	C

Reading Passage 3, Questions 27–40

27	B
28	E
29	A
30	C
31	G
32	TRUE
33	FALSE
34	TRUE
35	FALSE
36	NOT GIVEN
37	TRUE
38	FALSE
39	TRUE
40	NOT GIVEN

If you score . . .

0–12	13–29	30–40
you are unlikely to get an acceptable score under examination conditions and we recommend that you spend a lot of time improving your English before you take IELTS.	you may get an acceptable score under examination conditions but we recommend that you think about having more practice or lessons before you take IELTS.	you are likely to get an acceptable score under examination conditions but remember that different institutions will find different scores acceptable.

TEST 3

LISTENING

Section 1, Questions 1–10

1	Select
2	27.01.1973
3	15 Riverside
4	2 weeks
5	616295
6	engineer
7	mother
8	2,000
9	month
10	internet

Section 2, Questions 11–20

11	C
12	A
13	C
14	H
15	F
16	B
17	D
18	field
19	footbridge
20	viewpoint

Section 3, Questions 21–30

21	entertainment industry
22	telephone interviews
23	30/thirty
24	male and female
25	jazz
26	classical
27	concerts
28	department stores
29	club
30	opera house

Section 4, Questions 31–40

31	C
32	A
33	A
34	B
35	people
36	*IN EITHER ORDER*
	water
	sand
37	Scotland
38	outside
39	local
40	tops

If you score . . .

0–12	13–27	28–40
you are unlikely to get an acceptable score under examination conditions and we recommend that you spend a lot of time improving your English before you take IELTS.	you may get an acceptable score under examination conditions but we recommend that you think about having more practice or lessons before you take IELTS.	you are likely to get an acceptable score under examination conditions but remember that different institutions will find different scores acceptable.

ACADEMIC READING

Reading Passage 1, Questions 1–13

1 A
2 I
3 J
4 E
5 G
6 YES
7 NOT GIVEN
8 NOT GIVEN
9 NO
10 B
11 C
12 D
13 D

Reading Passage 2, Questions 14–27

14 vii
15 iii
16 ii
17 iv
18 i
19 NO
20 NOT GIVEN
21 NO
22 YES
23 NOT GIVEN
24 YES
25 B
26 C
27 A

Reading Passage 3, Questions 28–40

28 NO
29 YES
30 YES
31 NOT GIVEN
32 YES
33 A
34 B
35 C
36 A
37 B
38 glucose
39 free radicals
40 preservation

If you score . . .

0–11	12–28	29–40
you are unlikely to get an acceptable score under examination conditions and we recommend that you spend a lot of time improving your English before you take IELTS.	you may get an acceptable score under examination conditions but we recommend that you think about having more practice or lessons before you take IELTS.	you are likely to get an acceptable score under examination conditions but remember that different institutions will find different scores acceptable.

TEST 4

LISTENING

Section 1, Questions 1–10

1	75
2	cheque/check
3	15
4	25
5	10 minute(s')/min(s')
6	conference pack
7	South
8	library
9	5
10	21A

Section 2, Questions 11–20

11	D
12	A
13	C
14	tax
15	security
16	ground floor
17	lecture room 311
18	Safety at Work
19	Main Hall
20	team leaders

Section 3, Questions 21–30

21	reference
22	textbooks
23	secondary
24	primary
25	back
26	overdue books/ones
27	7 working days
28–30	*IN ANY ORDER*
	C
	E
	F

Section 4, Questions 31–40

31	B
32	A
33	B
34	C
35	1,450
36	disease
37	(wealthy) prince
38	diet
39	attack humans
40	leadership

If you score . . .

0–12	13–27	28–40
you are unlikely to get an acceptable score under examination conditions and we recommend that you spend a lot of time improving your English before you take IELTS.	you may get an acceptable score under examination conditions but we recommend that you think about having more practice or lessons before you take IELTS.	you are likely to get an acceptable score under examination conditions but remember that different institutions will find different scores acceptable.

ACADEMIC READING

Reading Passage 1, Questions 1–13

1	v
2	vi
3	iii
4	ix
5	i
6	vii
7	x
8	NO
9	YES
10	NO
11	YES
12	NOT GIVEN
13	YES

Reading Passage 2, Questions 14–26

14	B
15	F
16	C
17	J
18	F
19	NOT GIVEN
20	NO

21	YES
22	YES
23	NO
24	NOT GIVEN
25&26	***IN EITHER ORDER***
	C
	E

Reading Passage 3, Questions 27–40

27	iv
28	vi
29	v
30	vii
31	B
32	D
33	D
34	A
35	policy
36	(explicit) guidelines
37	(school) curriculum
38	victims
39	playful fighting
40	D

If you score . . .

0–12	13–29	30–40
you are unlikely to get an acceptable score under examination conditions and we recommend that you spend a lot of time improving your English before you take IELTS.	you may get an acceptable score under examination conditions but we recommend that you think about having more practice or lessons before you take IELTS.	you are likely to get an acceptable score under examination conditions but remember that different institutions will find different scores acceptable.

GENERAL TRAINING TEST A

READING

Section 1, Questions 1–14

1	B
2	F
3	D
4	A
5	FALSE
6	NOT GIVEN
7	NOT GIVEN
8	TRUE
9	TRUE
10	C
11	B
12	F
13	I
14	H

Section 2, Questions 15–27

15	B
16	G
17	F
18	E
19	A
20	F
21	G
22	C
23	B
24	A
25	A
26	B
27	B

Section 3, Questions 28–40

28	ix
29	vi
30	iv
31	ii
32	vii
33	viii
34	iii
35	prosperous
36	population
37	(modern) technology
38	leaks
39	management
40	water deficit

If you score . . .

0–17	18–29	30–40
you are unlikely to get an acceptable score under examination conditions and we recommend that you spend a lot of time improving your English before you take IELTS.	you may get an acceptable score under examination conditions but we recommend that you think about having more practice or lessons before you take IELTS.	you are likely to get an acceptable score under examination conditions but remember that different institutions will find different scores acceptable.

GENERAL TRAINING TEST B

READING

Section 1, Questions 1–14

1	***IN EITHER ORDER; BOTH REQUIRED FOR ONE MARK*** Saturday (and) Tuesday
2	***IN EITHER ORDER; BOTH REQUIRED FOR ONE MARK*** Saturday (and) Thursday
3	B
4	H
5	G
6	A
7	I
8	J
9	TRUE
10	NOT GIVEN
11	TRUE
12	TRUE
13	FALSE
14	FALSE

Section 2, Questions 15–27

15	xi
16	iv
17	v
18	ix
19	viii
20	ii
21	vii
22	K
23	C
24	I
25	H
26	G
27	L

Section 3, Questions 28–40

28	J
29	D
30	F
31	K
32	A
33	E
34	G
35	C
36	A
37	B
38	D
39	(over) a thousand
40	11 metres/meters

If you score . . .

0–16	17–28	29–40
you are unlikely to get an acceptable score under examination conditions and we recommend that you spend a lot of time improving your English before you take IELTS.	you may get an acceptable score under examination conditions but we recommend that you think about having more practice or lessons before you take IELTS.	you are likely to get an acceptable score under examination conditions but remember that different institutions will find different scores acceptable.

Model and sample answers for Writing tasks

TEST 1, WRITING TASK 1

MODEL ANSWER

This model has been prepared by an examiner as an example of a very good answer. However, please note that this is just one example out of many possible approaches.

> The graph shows how the amount of water used worldwide changed between 1900 and 2000.
>
> Throughout the century, the largest quantity of water was used for agricultural purposes, and this increased dramatically from about 500 km^3 to around 3,000 km^3 in the year 2000. Water used in the industrial and domestic sectors also increased, but consumption was minimal until mid-century. From 1950 onwards, industrial use grew steadily to just over 1,000 km^3, while domestic use rose more slowly to only 300 km^3, both far below the levels of consumption by agriculture.
>
> The table illustrates the differences in agricultural consumption in some areas of the world by contrasting the amount of irrigated land in Brazil (26,500 km^2) with that in the D.R.C. (100 km^2). This means that a huge amount of water is used in agriculture in Brazil, and this is reflected in the figures for water consumption per person: 359 m^3 compared with only 8 m^3 in the Congo. With a population of 176 million, the figures for Brazil indicate how high agricultural water consumption can be in some countries.

TEST 1, WRITING TASK 2

SAMPLE ANSWER

This is an answer written by a candidate who achieved a **Band 7.5** score. Here is the examiner's comment:

> The way in which the candidate has responded to the task is a strong point of this script. It is a well-developed answer that addresses the issues relevantly and at length. The writer introduces the topic, examines both sides of the argument and expresses a clear position. Points are well-argued and supported with examples.
>
> The answer is well-organised and the message is easy to follow with clear paragraphing and linking of ideas. There are too many errors in cohesion, however, and some linkers are not always fully appropriate, so this limits the rating for this criterion.
>
> A wide range of vocabulary is used accurately and precisely, in spite of one or two awkward expressions and some rare errors. Similarly, a sophisticated range of structures is used but there are too many minor errors and omissions (such as in the use of prepositions and basic subject/verb agreement) to reach Band 8. Nevertheless these mistakes do not reduce the clarity of the answer and overall a wide range of language is used with a high level of proficiency.

Nowadays, there are lots of advertisements on television or on the streets. Some people think that the advertising boosts the sales of goods and it encourages people to buy things unnecessarily. This arguments may be true. In my country, many advertising companies produce advertisements with famous and popular actors or singers. People, especially youngsters, buy goods that their favourite singer advertise, although they do not really need the products.

Also, on the television screen, a product may look gorgeous and good quality. As a result of it, people often buy goods without enough consideration. Consumers may not actually need it but they buy goods impulsively soon after they watch the advertising. Furthermore, as many customers buy a particular product due to its advertising campaign, the other people may be affected by the trend, even if the product is not of the real needs of the society.

On the other hand, there are various aspects against these arguments. Moreover, it is people's choice to make a decision to buy goods. Advertising may be not a cause of customers' buying habits. Individuals have their own spending habits. If they have got enough disposable income , then the right to make a decision is given to them. No one actually can judge whether the goods sold are the real needs of the society or not.

In addition, as there should be a limited amount of disposable income consumers are able to spend, people try to allocate their budgets. They cannot be simply swayed by those advertisements.

In conclusion, as customers have their own strong opinions and standard of good quality goods, it is better to leave them to make their own decision in buy goods. It is fairly difficult to say everyone is swayed by advertising and buy good impulsively. However, in sensitive area of businesses such as toy industries, it may be necessary to band advertising to those children as children have not got enough ability to control themselves or to know what they need.

TEST 2, WRITING TASK 1

SAMPLE ANSWER

This is an answer written by a candidate who achieved a **Band 6** score. Here is the examiner's comment:

> This answer does not introduce the information in the table, nor does it report it accurately. The figures are misinterpreted as representing the number of people rather than the average number of miles travelled per person per year. Consequently the information about the increase in total travel is simply not mentioned, so not all key information is covered. There is an attempt to summarise trends in the figures, but the reader cannot get a clear overall picture of the information because of the fundamental confusion.
>
> Nevertheless, the information is organised and the writing flows quite well because of good use of referencing and other connectors, but there are occasional errors in these and the links between ideas are slightly confusing at times.
>
> The strong feature in this answer is the range of vocabulary which is used with some flexibility and good control. A good range of structures is also used, but there are still some fairly basic mistakes, such as in the choice of tense, subject/verb agreement and inappropriate use of the passive.

In 2000 the most preferred mode of travel is by car with 4,806 people. There's a noticable decrease in public transportation locally where it dropped from 429 people in 1985 to 274 people in 2000. However the long distance bus rides is much more preferred by people as its figures are more than doubled in the last 15 years. People who chose to walk or cycle are decreased slightly in 2000. which probably made people to take the take the train more often. There's a significant increase in the numbers of people who travelled by train. It jumped from 289 in 1985 to 366 in 2000. This makes the train second popular mode of transportation. Thi biggest leap in the chart is the increase of taxi users who are tripled in 2000 with 42 people. where it was only 13 in 1985

Apart from all this modes of travel, there are some more different types of travel as well of course. Number of people choosing different modes of travel is rapidly increased from 450 to 585 in 2000.

TEST 2, WRITING TASK 2

MODEL ANSWER

This model has been prepared by an examiner as an example of a very good answer. However, please note that this is just one example out of many possible approaches.

As a result of constant media attention, sports professionals in my country have become stars and celebrities, and those at the top are paid huge salaries. Just like movie stars, they live extravagant lifestyles with huge houses and cars.

Many people find their rewards unfair, especially when comparing these super salaries with those of top surgeons or research scientists, or even leading politicians who have the responsibility of governing the country. However, sports salaries are not determined by considering the contribution to society a person makes, or the level of responsibility he or she holds. Instead, they reflect the public popularity of sport in general and the level of public support that successful stars can generate. So the notion of 'fairness' is not the issue.

Those who feel that sports stars' salaries are justified might argue that the number of professionals with real talent are very few, and the money is a recognition of the skills and dedication a person needs to be successful. Competition is constant and a player is tested every time they perform in their relatively short career. The pressure from the media is intense and there is little privacy out of the spotlight. So all of these factors may justify the huge earnings.

Personally, I think that the amount of money such sports stars make is more justified than the huge earnings of movie stars, but at the same time, it indicates that our society places more value on sport than on more essential professions and achievements.

TEST 3, WRITING TASK 1

MODEL ANSWER

This model has been prepared by an examiner as an example of a very good answer. However, please note that this is just one example out of many possible approaches.

The first diagram shows that there are four main stages in the life of the silkworm. First of all, eggs are produced by the moth and it takes ten days for each egg to become a silkworm larva that feeds on mulberry leaves. This stage lasts for up to six weeks until the larva produces a cocoon of silk thread around itself. After a period of about three weeks, the adult moths eventually emerge from these cocoons and the life cycle begins again.

The cocoons are the raw material used for the production of silk cloth. Once selected, they are boiled in water and the threads can be separated in the unwinding stage. Each thread is between 300 and 900 metres long, which means they can be twisted together, dyed and then used to produce cloth in the weaving stage.

Overall, the diagrams show that the cocoon stage of the silkworm can be used to produce silk cloth through a very simple process.

TEST 3, WRITING TASK 2

SAMPLE ANSWER

This is an answer written by a candidate who achieved a **Band 4** score. Here is the examiner's comment:

> This answer is considerably underlength at 186 words and it loses marks for this. The writing tries to address the two points of view in the question, but it is so underlength that main ideas are not developed enough. The writer expresses a point of view, but this is not always clear for the reader.
>
> There is a certain logic to the way the ideas are organised, and a range of logical connectors is used. However, these connectives are often inaccurate and at times it is difficult to understand the relationship between the points.
>
> Control of vocabulary is weak and the errors in word form and spelling make it hard for the reader to understand the message at times. Phrases from the question are copied directly, even when inappropriate, and this reveals the limitations in the writer's vocabulary. Similarly, there is poor control of grammatical structures, with mistakes in even simple sentences. Although there are occasional accurate structures, the number of mistakes causes great strain for the reader.

In the Recent years, between the different countries, a lof of people keen on visit to other countries. Those peope like to learn the different cultural and reconize different things from the other countries.

In my opinion, every host country should welcome cultural differences. Because the visitors were stay a short time for their journey. They will travel and shopping in the cities. Sometime, they can bring up the cultural and enconomoic were development. Althought, the language and the lifestyle are different, but we shall learn from ... their lanuage.

Some people cannot accept the visitors. I think they afair to effect the local customs. And ... the don't the visitors behaviour were effect to their countries saft. Therefore the cannot accept. The visitors might be the crime and escept from their countries. However, they afaird the visitors whose will destronye their counties.

In summerise, the people should accept the host country and welcome cultural differences. They will earn a lot for other countries. such as cultural, reglious, knowledge, Arts etc, If they can accept the other countries visitors. They might be benefit a lot than they needs.

TEST 4, WRITING TASK 1

SAMPLE ANSWER

This is an answer written by a candidate who achieved a **Band 6.5** score. Here is the examiner's comment:

> The Task Achievement is the weak point in this answer. Some of the data is summarised but the points are not well-selected to convey the key trends shown in the charts. The main features of the first chart are not adequately presented and the overall conclusion does not summarise the main information. No figures are given to illustrate the points made.
>
> The information is well-organised, however, with clear paragraphing and well-signalled sections. The accurate use of a range of sequencers and other linkers makes it easy to follow the writing. There are examples of errors but they are not frequent and do not cause confusion.
>
> A range of vocabulary is used with flexibility, in spite of some inappropriate collocations and awkward phrasing. Structures are varied and generally accurate, while any mistakes do not make the message unclear.

We are given two charts which show us a few sets of data about the marital status of the Americans between 1970 and 2000.

The first chart compares the number of marriages and divorces in the United States of America between 1970 and 2000. We can see that data is given for each decade; the number of people who are getting married decreased slightly since 1980, as well as the divorces one. Nevertheless, divorces increased between 1970 and 1980.

The second chart is more precise about the different marital status of the Americans between 1970 and 2000. The number of divorced people has risen more than the double during this two years, and the data for the never married people has also increased significantly. However, less and less people are married, as the first chart showed us; the widowed American number is also decreasing.

As a conclusion, we can say that the marital status background of the Americans has maybe known the greatest change it had ever seen.

TEST 4, WRITING TASK 2

MODEL ANSWER

This model has been prepared by an examiner as an example of a very good answer. However, please note that this is just one example out of many possible approaches.

Over the last half century the pace of change in the life of human beings has increased beyond our wildest expectations. This has been driven by technological and scientific breakthroughs that are changing the whole way we view the world on an almost daily basis. This means that change is not always a personal option, but an inescapable fact of life, and we need to constantly adapt to keep pace with it.

Those people who believe they have achieved some security by doing the same, familiar things are living in denial. Even when people believe they are resisting change themselves, they cannot stop the world around them from changing. Sooner or later they will find that the familiar jobs no longer exist, or that the 'safe' patterns of behaviour are no longer appropriate.

However, reaching the conclusion that change is inevitable is not the same as assuming that 'change is always for the better'. Unfortunately, it is not always the case that new things are promoted because they have good impacts for the majority of people. A lot of innovations are made with the aim of making money for a few. This is because it is the rich and powerful people in our society who are able to impose changes (such as in working conditions or property developments) that are in their own interests.

In conclusion, I would say that change can be stimulating and energising for individuals when they pursue it themselves, but that all change, including that which is imposed on people, does not necessarily have good outcomes.

TEST A, WRITING TASK 1 (GENERAL TRAINING)

MODEL ANSWER

This model has been prepared by an examiner as an example of a very good answer. However, please note that this is just one example out of many possible approaches.

Dear Mr Smith,

I am your tenant from Flat 3 on Riverside Street. We met each other when I signed the rental agreement in your office.

I have lived here for 6 months now and I am writing to complain about some of the furniture. As you may remember, the dining table is in very poor condition and has uneven legs. It also does not match the dining chairs as these are too low to be comfortable for a table of that height. When I first pointed this out to you, you agreed to provide a brand new dining set. However, you have not done so and I would really like to resolve this matter as soon as possible.

If it is more convenient for you, perhaps you could simply replace the table by finding one of a suitable height for the chairs. This would solve the problems without too much cost, so I hope you agree to this proposed solution.

Looking forward to hearing from you,

Yours sincerely,

M.M. Egil

TEST A, WRITING TASK 2 (GENERAL TRAINING)

SAMPLE ANSWER

This is an answer written by a candidate who achieved a **Band 6** score. Here is the examiner's comment:

> This answer has a clear focus and presents a very definite point of view about the general topic area. However, the second question is not directly addressed and no identifiable parenting skills are described. This means the task is only partially answered and this limits the Band score.
>
> The argument is quite easy to follow and a range of devices is used to connect the ideas. However, some of these connectives are not appropriate and paragraphing is not always logical, especially at the beginning of the answer. The closing statement in the conclusion is relevant to the argument but it is not well integrated into the writing.
>
> A range of vocabulary is used with flexibility and a good level of control. There are examples of appropriate idiomatic expressions that suggest that the writer has a good active resource. There are some lapses and some minor spelling mistakes, but these do not reduce communication.
>
> The writer uses a range of structures effectively and accurately, with examples of sophisticated phrasing. However, there are quite a lot of short, simple sentences too, and there are lapses and omissions in some structures, although these do not prevent the reader from understanding the message.

Every young person, male or female should know more about being a good parent before having children. There are many cases in which very young women give birth to little babies, without having a clue what means to be a parent.

In addition, school should provide courses, teaching young persons to be good parents. It might seem as something very easy. Every woman can be a mother, the problem is what kind of mother she is.

It is said that human instinct develops after giving birth to a child and every mother – father instinctually feels what to do for the baby. But, there are some things that ought to be known before.

A child is not a simple toy. A child is a big responsability, love and care. A mother should know if she is ready or not to have a child, and a couple should prepare before having children.

We can see many cases with families behaving badly – in real life, on TV, reading newspapers, when children are very bad, when parents abuse their olnly children, screaming and shouting, smacking them. Who is guilty then? The parent or the child? This cases can end really badly if the persons in charge – here – parents and not the children – don't learn how to behave themselves, how to handle their children, how and when to give them support.

In addition to all the things written above, it would be a very good idea for schools to teach young persons become good parents, as this can help young people how to to handle their own problems and above all their children's problems.

A child is the mirror of the parents.

TEST B, WRITING TASK 1 (GENERAL TRAINING)

SAMPLE ANSWER

This is an answer written by a candidate who achieved a **Band 6** score. Here is the examiner's comment:

> The letter has a clear purpose and all the information required in the task is provided and well-extended by the writer. The tone is consistently informal and friendly, which suits the situation. The closing expression is over-formal and adds an inappropriate tone, but this is only a minimal lapse in the whole response.
>
> The information is generally organised throughout the letter, but while there are one or two examples of good linking, there is a lot of omission, and 'also' is used rather repetitively. As a result, sentences are not fluently linked and this limits the rating.
>
> Vocabulary is adequate and appropriate for the task although the range is not wide. The level of control is generally good with only a few spelling mistakes. The range of structures is limited and repetitive, however. There are one or two examples of complex structures used well, but overall there are lots of simple clauses that have inaccurate punctuation. This is a weak point of this answer.

Dear neighbour,

I am your new neighbour, I moved in Last week with my son, I am working as a nurse in the nearby hospital. I am planning to hold a party, I will invite all my friends and relatives, my son also will invite his friends I would like to invite yu too, I will be happy to see you.

At the party I will provide all kind of drinks, different type of food, I will prepare intercontinental dishes as well as some Arabic food, in addition I will also get some Indian and chinese food , I will order them from the restaurant, so we will have planty of food and drinks, we will also listen to some music and I will introduced you to all of my ferinds, also who ever likes to dance they can. I hope everyone will enjoy the party and have fun including you.

If you decided not to come for any reason, please inform me, and I want to be sure that the noise will not disturb you.

Looking forward to see you, as this party gives both of us the opportunity to be good freinds.

yours faithfully,

Mahir

TEST B, WRITING TASK 2 (GENERAL TRAINING)

MODEL ANSWER

This model has been prepared by an examiner as an example of a very good answer. However, please note that this is just one example out of many possible approaches.

I tend to agree that young children can be negatively affected by too much time spent on the computer every day. This is partly because sitting in front of a screen for too long can be damaging to both the eyes and the physical posture of a young child, regardless of what they are using the computer for.

However, the main concern is about the type of computer activities that attract children. These are often electronic games that tend to be very intense and rather violent. The player is usually the 'hero' of the game and too much exposure can encourage children to be self-centred and insensitive to others.

Even when children use a computer for other purposes, such as getting information or emailing friends, it is no substitute for human interaction. Spending time with other children and sharing non-virtual experiences is an important part of a child's development that cannot be provided by a computer.

In spite of this, the obvious benefits of computer skills for young children cannot be denied. Their adult world will be changing constantly in terms of technology and the Internet is the key to all the knowledge and information available in the world today. Therefore it is important that children learn at an early age to use the equipment enthusiastically and with confidence as they will need these skills throughout their studies and working lives.

I think the main point is to make sure that young children do not overuse computers. Parents must ensure that their children learn to enjoy other kinds of activity and not simply sit at home, learning to live in a virtual world.

Sample answer sheets

BRITISH COUNCIL **IELTS AUSTRALIA** **UNIVERSITY *of* CAMBRIDGE ESOL Examinations**

PENCIL must be used to complete this sheet

Centre number:

Please write your name below,

then write your six digit Candidate number in the boxes
and shade the number in the grid on the right in PENCIL.

0 1 2 3 4 5 6 7 8 9
0 1 2 3 4 5 6 7 8 9
0 1 2 3 4 5 6 7 8 9
0 1 2 3 4 5 6 7 8 9
0 1 2 3 4 5 6 7 8 9
0 1 2 3 4 5 6 7 8 9

Test date (shade ONE box for the day, ONE box for the month and ONE box for the year):

Day: 01 02 03 04 05 06 07 08 09 10 11 12 13 14 15 16 17 18 19 20 21 22 23 24 25 26 27 28 29 30 31

Month: 01 02 03 04 05 06 07 08 09 10 11 12 Last 2 digits of the **Year**: 00 01 02 03 04 05 06 07 08 09

IELTS Listening Answer Sheet

#		✓ X	#		✓ X
1		1	21		21
2		2	22		22
3		3	23		23
4		4	24		24
5		5	25		25
6		6	26		26
7		7	27		27
8		8	28		28
9		9	29		29
10		10	30		30
11		11	31		31
12		12	32		32
13		13	33		33
14		14	34		34
15		15	35		35
16		16	36		36
17		17	37		37
18		18	38		38
19		19	39		39
20		20	40		40

Checker's Initials	Marker's Initials	Band Score	Listening Total

IELTS L-R v4.0   DP500/392

Sample answer sheets

Are you: Female? ▭   Male? ▭

Your first language code: ▶ 0 1 2 3 4 5 6 7 8 9
   ▶ 0 1 2 3 4 5 6 7 8 9
   ▶ 0 1 2 3 4 5 6 7 8 9

IELTS Reading Answer Sheet

Module taken (shade one box):   Academic ▭   General Training ▭

		✓ ✗			✓ ✗
1		✓ 1 ✗	**21**		✓ 21 ✗
2		2	**22**		22
3		3	**23**		23
4		4	**24**		24
5		5	**25**		25
6		6	**26**		26
7		7	**27**		27
8		8	**28**		28
9		9	**29**		29
10		10	**30**		30
11		11	**31**		31
12		12	**32**		32
13		13	**33**		33
14		14	**34**		34
15		15	**35**		35
16		16	**36**		36
17		17	**37**		37
18		18	**38**		38
19		19	**39**		39
20		20	**40**		40

Checker's Initials		Marker's Initials		Band Score		Reading Total	

Acknowledgements

The authors and publishers are grateful to the following for permission to reproduce copyright material. While every effort has been made, it has not always been possible to identify the sources of all the material used, or to contact the copyright holders. If any omissions are brought to our notice, we will be happy to include the appropriate acknowledgements on reprinting.

The publishers are grateful to the following for permission to reproduce copyright material:

For the text on pp. 18–19: 'Australia's Sporting Success' by Wilson da Silva, *New Scientist*, 26 January 2002, for the text on pp. 27–28 'Climate Change and the Inuit' by Sue Armstrong, *New Scientist*, November 2001, for the text on pp. 44–45: 'Greying Population stays in the Pink', by Philip Cohen, *New Scientist*, 16 March 2004, for the text on pp. 89–90: 'Do literate women make better mothers?' by H Epstein, *New Scientist*, 29 April 1995. Used by permission of New Scientist; for the text on pp. 22–23: 'Delivering the goods'. *The Economist* 13 November 1997. © The Economist Newspaper, Limited, London; for the text on pp. 41–42: 'Advantages of public transport', by Stephen Luntz. *Australasian Science*, August 1998. Used by permission of Auspac Media Pty Ltd; for the text on pp. 48–49: 'Numeration' by Michael Williams. Taken from *A History of Computing Technology*. © 1997. Reprinted with permission of John Wiley & Sons, Inc; for the text on pp. 68–69: 'Motivating employees under adverse conditions'. Reproduced from Robbins & Mukerji *Managing Organisations: New challenges and perspectives (2nd edition)*. © Pearson Education Australia, 1994; for the text on pp. 71–72: 'The search for the anti-aging pill' by M Lane, D Ingram and G Roth. *Scientific American*, 16 July 2002. Used by permission of Scientific American, Inc. All rights reserved; for the text on pp. 86–87: 'Doctoring Sales' by Erin Strout. *Sales and Marketing Management*, May 2001. Used by permission of VNU Business Media, Inc; for the text on pp. 94–95: 'Bullying' by Peter Smith. *Children UK*, Winter 1994. Reproduced with the kind permission of the National Children's Bureau; for the text on pp. 110–111: 'The Water Crisis' taken from *Understanding Global Issues*. © 2001. Used by permission of European Schoolbooks Ltd; for the text on pp. 122–124: 'Pterosaurs' taken from *National Geographic*, May 2001. © Richard Monastersky/National Geographic Image Collection.

The publishers are grateful to the following for permission to include photographs:
p. 18; p. 27; p. 41; p. 48; p. 89; p. 110: Corbis; p. 122 Natural History Museum.

Design concept by Peter Ducker MSTD

Cover design by John Dunne

The cassettes and audio CDs which accompany this book were recorded at Studio AVP, London.

Page make up by Servis Filmsetting Ltd.